A Dualistic Industrial Relations

# Industrial Relations-
# Theoretical Perspective

By

**B Mathew**

**First Edition**

# Industrial Relations- Theoretical Perspective

By

**B Mathew**

ISBN: 9781656376305



**Published by**
**Amazon USA**

# About the author

**B Mathew**-  a human resources practitioner for last 25 years, has previously worked for large unionized, high volume manufacturing companies as Head of Human Resources & Industrial Relations and has successfully handled & managed national union strikes, lock-outs & Collective Agreement negotiations. He has also represented employers in Industrial Courts and labour courts on dismissal cases. He is currently a Human Resources Consultant.

He is a prolific writer, author and publisher with Amazon.

# 1

## Introduction to Industrial Relations

### Evolution

In a simple one to one employment relation between an employee and employer we do not use the word industrial relations. We merely use the term- employee-employer relations. The term, industrial relations carries a connotation of a formal relationship of high or extreme complexity index. Having its root in historical evolution during the Industrial Revolution in Europe between the periods 1780 - 1850 which brought about unprecedented economic boom to the Western World. Where heretofore dormant and low profile manufacturing activity took a colossal leap and preeminence over agriculture, commerce, banking, trading and services, in the technological changes whereof saw the rise of complex factory organization, industrial engineering techniques, specialization of skills akin to factory labour and high volume labour intensive mass production which resulted in more lateral distribution of wealth and the rise of proletariat working class.

### The Historical Perspective Of the Industrial Revolution

The Industrial Revolution was birth and cradled in Great Britain during the 18th century where prior to this, it consisted of mostly an agrarian society, with craftsmen manning primitive domestic low-volume manufacturing activities housed in shady homes, cottages and makeshift huts and small shops using simple hand-tools and indigenous equipment. In the absence of buoyant trade, business and commerce including reasonable earnings, life and livelihood of most people were simple and one of self-sufficiency as they endeavored to provide their own foods, clothes, shelter and tools. But Britain was a great nation and a world power and was a leading colonial power during this era. Britain had access to huge reserves of raw materials in these colonial nations in addition to possessing huge reserves of coal and iron ore in its own soil. The climate was right and ripe for a gargantuan thrust into manufacturing activity as Britain saw the potential of a huge oversea market in these colonial nations. Thus the advent of Industrialization in Britain, which later spread across to Germany, France and Belgium and thereafter to the United States. Some of the key industries affected by this revolution in Britain were textiles, iron and steel which took a giant leap forward from small scale primitive low volume production to high volume, high tech mass production.

Textiles for example, were traditionally spun at home in slow pace, mainly for domestic and family consumption, and its production was mainly relied upon skills of artisans. But with the introduction of spinning-jenny by a Scottish inventor, various textile products were rolled out en-mass in high volume with almost negligible reliance on artisans or on human energy. The spinning equipment or jenny as it was called then, could be easily handled by non-skilled labor. As demand for textile products further surged exponentially, the spinning-jenny gave way to an improved version of technological innovation called the spinning-mule which rolled out textile products at an even greater speed and better quality. By now it was no longer crude domestic output but rather large scale factory output en-mass employing sophisticated industrial engineering scheduling and other high powered techniques. Masses of unskilled labour were engaged as machine operatives in round the clock shifts.

The iron and steel industries, another key factor in the new industrial revival underwent complete transformation and contributed to modernization of infrastructure, buildings, shipping and to new machines, while steam technology gave cheap power to run locomotives, ships, machines and plants that were generating myriad new manufacturing products which were then transported across the oceans by newly built large steam-powered freight ships to satisfy massive oversea demand for British goods.

And fueling this revival fires of industrialization was a Scottish economist, Adam Smith, who came out with his popular philosophy, "The Wealth Of The Nation" promoting free enterprise with negligible government interference and private ownership of business and wealth.

**Complexity Index Of Industrial Relations**
And adding to this complexity index are wholesale influx of trade union laws, industrial relations regulating laws, labour laws, occupational safety laws and social security laws as mass conversion of iron, steel, rubber, cotton, clay, sands and other

primary raw materials brought international trade and international business dealing to dizzy heights thus further resulting in the development of international trade laws and international labour regulatory laws to regulate, manage and monitor global labour & trade union movement, industrial relation and social changes. Industrial relations as what appears today following its massive evolvement from its historical roots are a set of employment practices, laws and norms governing and regulating harmonious relationship between two antagonistic entities like trade union of workers one hand  and employers or trade union of employers on other hand with diametrically opposed goals and objectives, of various industries amongst others including manufacturing, oil & gas, agriculture, mining, banking, commerce, services, shipping and transport with the government playing a mediatory role. Thus the key players in this index, modelled after Anglo – Saxon array, are the employers, employees and the governments with each having diverse and antagonistic interests and agenda but having a tripartite nexus with one another.

The concept of industrial relations, what began as strictly labour relations encompassing primarily only unionized workers against a backdrop of large unionized manufacturing setting slowly incorporated in the passing of time other non-manufacturing sectors both unionized and non-unionized sectors:

- Thus **medieval Industrial Relations** included only labour relations of unionized manufacturing sectors,

- **Neo-classical Industrial Relations** included employer-employee relations of both unionized and non-unionized business sectors,

- And **modern day Industrial Relations** evolved to embrace additional elements of human resources management, organization behavior and conflict management in both unionized and non-unionized business sectors.

Adding further to this complexity index would be the theoretical perception of industrial relations as viewed by three schools of scholarly thoughts and they are namely:

- The Dualistic School of industrial relations,

- The Unitaristic School of industrial relations,

- The Classical or Marxist School of Industrial relations.

**The Classical or Marxist School of Industrial relations**
The Classical school sees employers as capitalists and therefore inherently exploitative in nature. And because of this underlying antagonism, workplace conflict, industrial disputes and union formation are causal response. In contrast to the Unitaristic school, a clear demarcation is drawn between capitalistic employers and exploited workers. Where this school of thought perceives a perpetual and unceasing struggle between the two entities, with employers wielding an upper-hand over the workers as the former is invariably inclined towards creation of monopoly and the suppression of workers' wages. This school sees workplace conflict as perennial animosity between capital and labour resulting from inequality of bargaining power, an obvious bane in any capitalistic society and its laissez-faire economy, as especially in a state of negligible control by government.

**The Dualistic School of industrial relations**
The Dualistic school perceives industrial relations as positive interaction between two main protagonists, that is, the employer on one hand and the trade union of workers on the other, with both entities considered as almost of equal standing and where clear demarcation is drawn between these two entities in respect of their respective aspiration, goals, objectives and agenda. And that conflict between the two is inherent, natural and unavoidable but is taken objectively on a positive premise of compromise, encouragement and mutual cooperation where the trade union of workers is taken as positive, beneficial and accepted as legitimate representative body by the employer. In the same token unionized workers also accept the employer and is accorded the same loyalty and respect as the union. Where bilateral accord can be attained by collective bargaining based on mutual understanding of respective rights, entitlement, interest and motives. Industrial disputes are formally settled or resolved amicably by way of governmental intervention through conciliatory or arbitration bodies. Employers are encouraged to hire and rely on industrial relations specialists to minimize workplace conflict and to accord the union due recognition through appropriate communication,

negotiation and consultation. Where Collective Agreements are treated as primary document and is an important source in resolving all and any workplace conflict which may arise and is therefore incumbent upon both workers and employers to strictly comply with its provision.

**The Unitaristic School of industrial relations**
The Unitaristic school as diametrically opposed to the Dualistic school sees industrial relations only through the unilateral eyes of the employer and hence views the workers' union in negative glance, in particular, abhorrence for any dissenting views or disputes coming from workers. As proponent of paternalistic philosophy, the employer as paternal head of family with upper hand demands and expects total loyalty from the workers in consideration of its guarantee of workers livelihood, sustenance and welfare. Where both employer and the workers are looked upon as a single entity having the same single aspiration and sharing the same single goals, objective and interest and therefore the Union is not recognized neither has the Union any part in this family unit. In the underlying unison goal where the employer's primary goals are invariably forged with the workers' through regular discourse and integrated programmes of mutual benefits. And adding to the foregoing discourse and integrated programmes should be the workers' remuneration package and reward system ingeniously designed so as to extract voluntary dedication, goodwill, enthusiasm and cooperation from the workers.   It sees workplace conflict as mere communication breakdown between management and workers and employs informal means to resolve this breach.

From the corridors of time since its advent during the great Industrial Revolution in the west including that of the United States of America which saw great and mighty union movements and its proliferation thereof, of which the philosophy of the Classical / Marxist school of Industrial Relations was not only at the height of notoriety but also in prominence, there were some undercurrents of paradigm shifts that were surely but subtly corroding away the fundamental structure of archaic or classical industrial relations. From its transition from Classical stage to Dualistic stage and thereafter to Unitaristic stage, these subtle undercurrents led to a slow decline of unions and worker representation by trade unions over time. This structural decline was in fact due to in deference to emerging trend of new meta-theories of industrial relations that analyzed and promulgated labor-empowerment philosophies which excited not only labor on one hand but equally excited capitalism as well on the other finale. Going back to the roots from where it all began, both Capitalism and labor with respective diversity of interests, motives and agenda and opposed to each other began converging together in business endeavors and that was where the inception of Industrial Relations flourished and boomeranged. But what undermined this structure and brought about the downfall and decline of unions? But before this, let us look at the following report by STAR:

MTUC: Only 9% of workers in Malaysia unionised

Sunday, 12 Feb 2012
12:00 AM MYT

KUALA LUMPUR: A mere nine per cent of the nation's 11 million workers are unionised and this figure is far from that of nations like Japan, the United Kingdom and Singapore.

A total 18% of workers in Singapore are in trade unions while the figure stands at 21% and 29% for Japan and the United Kingdom, respectively.

"This percentage has never gone up and has been at the same level for the past few decades. We still face a lot of challenges in forming unions, and compared to many Asian countries, we are still far down," Malaysian Trades Union Congress (MTUC) vice-president A. Balasubramaniam said in an interview.

He cautioned that the number of workers joining trade unions was on the decline while the population and the opportunities for work were on a steady rise.

Balasubramaniam said the Government, especially the ministry, must recognise the need for workers to be unionised as this was not only good for workers but also employers.

"Once a company is formed and has more than a number of workers, the workers should be allowed to form auto unions. This means the union is automatically formed without having to get the permission of the employer," he added.

He urged the ministry to take proactive steps in encouraging effective unionism in the country.

A Dualistic Industrial Relations



Let us now consider some of the these undercurrent paradigm shifts, which steered the once formidable union movement to its present worldwide debilitation and namely the paradigm shifts of,

- Workers empowerment notion and

- Employers' social accountabilities notion

- Fresh repertoires for labour representation.

**Workers Empowerment Notion**
The term "Workers Empowerment" or "Workers High Performance Work Systems" or any other nascent programmes akin to employee empowerment methods could be interchangeably used to refer the same or similar idea or methodology. Going back to yonder years of classical epoch, where workers faced-off intimidating employers, where these employers had no other statutory, moral or ethical obligation or restrain otherwise than to maximize organizational profit and its monetary and business growth at all cost, thereby turning a blind eye to the rampant and obvious exploitation in terms of low wages, long and brutal working hours, unsafe working environment, unsecure employment tenure under prevailing harshness of common laws with negligible government intervention, the critical institutions of unions and collective agreement emerged with the right to worker representations, to withhold labour and the right to strike and to counter-balance the ruthlessness of the employers.

Herein lays the root of all industrial dispute between capitalist employers and laboring workers which feeds the empowerment of unionism:

On one hand, the entrepreneurs only perceive workers as mere chattel, disposable at will at any time for any reason and are only obsessed with maximizing profits by way of expending lowest wage cost as possible and exacting maximum working hours from workers while on other hand the laboring workers want to earn maximum wages at minimum working hours with fullest security of tenure. (Was it not for this very reason during the foregoing era of the Great Industrial Revolution the working class were exploited with low wages and brutally long hours and without security of tenure, replaceable at will. Child labor was rampant, with pollution and unsanitary living conditions which were breeding grounds for plague and disease. And over-crowded and deplorable housing for outstation laborers who converged at industrialized city-centers. These were the fruits of Adam Smith's philosophy especially when it negated and curtailed governmental intervention especially during early and mid-era of the Industrial Revolution in Great Britain).

This prevailing antagonistic goals and objectives, of capitalistic employers and laboring workers which are diametrically opposed to each other was soon impinged upon by labour-empowerment ideas through rational reasoning that persuaded both entities to rather than reckoning laboring workers as mere chattel or machine to view and consider them as potential resources instead having the intrinsic seed or germination of greatness that waits to be harnessed.

For example, if a worker breaches his contract of service by poor, **unsatisfactory job performance**, classical industrial relations says that the employer should hold an inquiry and punish him via warning or a suspension or even by way of a dismissal for the said breach of the required benchmark. And this dispute is what actually empowers union, as the worker has no other alternative but to seek union representation to aid him in this dispute. But the Worker Empowerment Notion says you should not treat this matter as a dispute but inject the necessary training to correct and strengthen his weak areas so as to lift him up to the required benchmark of job performance because humans have the capacity to learn and acquire new and additional skills as compared to an inert chattel.

Unsatisfactory work performance of a worker results when there is a void of specialization, and instead the focus is wrongly directed towards MULTI-TASKING SKILLS as taught by our modern human resources gurus. Consider the hypothetical case below:

## A MULTI-TASKING CAT TAKES A GRAB-RIDE HOME

Imagine the misery of an old worker who had spent the last 40 years acquiring skills in operating printing machines in the printing industry, suddenly becoming redundant when his Company closes down. Another prospective employer enquires if he can handle a hydraulic press in the ceramic industry! Well, if he can't, then blame the old worker for not acquiring multi-tasking skills offered by our HR trainers.

Imagine an old, experienced doctor who had spent the last 40 years practicing medicine suddenly becoming redundant and goes out of job! Well, if he can't do an engineer's job, then blame the doctor for not acquiring multi-tasking skills in engineering offered by our HR trainers.   Well, if Multi-Tasking is indeed effective, then the case of a Cat taking a Grab-ride home would become a possibility.

Another example, if a worker is inclined to get into frequent argument with his supervisor and shows his proclivity to abhor any forms of scrutiny by his superiors under his contract of service, the classical industrial relations dictates that the said worker should be punished for **insubordination**, since such refusal to take orders from superiors would be deemed a misdemeanor and a breach of his contract of service with the employer.  The again, the Workers' Empowerment Notion says it would be very wrong to subject the said worker to scrutiny or supervision, instead the employer should give such worker considerable autonomy, encouragement and motivation in performing his task, where necessary with bare minimum supervision. Because, this would waken, quicken and revive the dead, dormant and sleeping talents, skills and sleeping creativity within him to become instead a paragon of shining success, thus benefiting the employer.

Thus evolving further and further we now behold the foregoing empowerment notion totally debilitating the union and its fundamental role of labor representation as workers now receive and enjoy more and more discretionary and decision-making powers granted by employers in running their business, production and service operations akin to de-facto business partnership.  Where workers reaping emotional, psychological viz mental and egotistic, and financial fulfillment and rewards resulting from this de-facto partnership with employers will now inadvertently steer clear of erstwhile industrial disputes and conflicts with employers, which being a disreputable pattern of classical epoch which affected deleteriously not only the employers, the workers and the government but also the whole business, economic, political and social climate.

**Corporate Social Responsibility Notion**
The notion of social solidarity , was a notion initially mooted by unions which took an extra mile or a detour from their core duties like worker representation, collective agreement negotiation, handling trade dispute issues and other myriad matters akin to core industrial relations callings, to venture into unchartered expanses of social accountability and take upon themselves voluntarily what would be otherwise ethical and moral responsibilities without any compulsion from any legal enforcement bodies, to be actively involved in workers' welfare programmes, community projects and family activities that would positively and benevolently impact not only workers and employees but also the  families, communities and the whole social structure at large. By these noble acts, the union was digging deeper its heel and reinforcing itself as a sole champion of workers' cause against the employer. And the labour force in seeing this nobility, held the union in high veneration. But later this noble responsibility or calling, or what was even reckoned a sole bounden calling of the union, was usurped by employers, who then took upon themselves another bounden calling which became magnanimously known as **Corporate-Social-Responsibility** (CSR).

Let us take a look at this corporate social responsibility within the Malaysian context during the decades of 1950's and 1960's and even the spans preceding and succeeding this. The ideals and early models of corporate social responsibility first began and was exhibited in the plantation sector and in particular within estates in then Malaya managed by British and European household agencies, which were amongst others Guthrie, Socfin, Harrison & Crossfield and United Plantations.

Where these employers assumed not only the responsibility of the hiring of direct migrant labourers from India but also a sense of moral and ethical duty:

- To permit these migrant labourers to bring along their wives and children,

- To provide reasonable housing facilities for migrant labourers and their dependents,

- To provide estate hospitals and trained & qualified estate hospital assistants and mid-wives to treat these migrant labourers and their dependents including child deliveries,

- To provide estate nursery centers for migrant labourers' children,

- To provide and built estate schools for migrant labourers school going children,

- To erect temples and provided  prayer & worship facilities for these migrant labourers and their families,

- To provide children's playground in estates including recreational fields, facilities for adults including open-air movie screenings.

- Not to mentioned legalized booze shops for drinking adults.

The foregoing social altruism, a striking archetypal seen in plantation sector would deter or even minimize to a consideration extent crime rates, social problems, delinquencies and violence. And the labor force in perceiving this variety of social altruism displayed by employers, then began unconsciously and inadvertently venerating these employers as well just like the union, thereby beginning a transition from classical to dualistic industrial relations.

Corporate social responsibility and the abbreviation CRS, or even going by a heightened term, which is more refined and namely, **Employer's Social Altruism** or going by the acronym of **ESA**, has indeed a constructive impact on social solidarity due to a underlying nexus with it. This underlying bond being that ESA would bring down or destroy any forms of adverse psychological strongholds of animosity, antagonism and damaging perception of the employer the employee might have or wont to have or possess, thus enticing the employee to take closer steps to the employer. What brought about or goaded the transition from classical industrial relations epoch, where so to say for our illustration, when employers and employees were ten miles apart from each other? Or down to the dualistic epoch where so to say for our illustration, when employers and employees were merely two miles apart from each other? Or further down to the Unitaristic epoch when employers and employees were embracing each other in such close partnership?  Was it not **Employer's Social Altruism,** which actually brought down these barriers of separation, drawing these two opposed entities which were miles apart erstwhile, closer together, while the prominence of trade unionism plummeted down.

But what do we see today? Social Malignance. Today's Malaysian employers usually cram foreign workers into small shoddy rooms which is more befitting animals or modern day slaves. And these foreign workers are not allowed to bring their families, wives, and children or allowed to marry locals. Most of these foreign workers are singles and they are required to only labour long hours in factories or construction sites, without fulfilling their mental, emotional and other physical needs.

Perhaps this provides answers to why present day foreign workers in Malaysia, the Bangla, the Nepalese, the Vietnamese and the other foreigners are involved in sexual crimes, other criminal activities and all forms of unhealthy social activities.

Present day foreign workers are expected

- to work long hours,

- work on rest day,

- are not supposed to fall sick or take medical leaves,

- are supposed to be more hard-working than locals,

- are supposed to work with minimum safety gears.

If they fall short of these expectations, then they face prospect of dismissal. If this is the plight of legalize, documented foreigner workers, just imagine what would be the plight of undocumented illegal foreign workers.)

**Fresh repertoires for labour representation.**
In sum, traditional repertoires of labour representation are actually institutionalized undertakings like the whole spectrum of tasks discharged by the entity of union- handling trade-disputes, non-compliance matters, dismissal cases, collective-agreement negotiation including court cognizance thereof, industrial strikes and stand-off with employers in a push for workers' cause and the transpiration of which takes place within the precincts of embedded formal, legal settings. But take the example of the fresh, new and contemporary repertoires of "labour representation" that is totally void of the entity of the union and that which transpires without the precincts of any embedded legal or formal settings, mounting informal pressure on employers for any perpetrated injustice, unfairness or exploitation inflicted upon labour force. Especially when such workers' cause is promulgated by non-government bodies, welfare groups, bar council or legal aid bureau  by way of social media, street protest and TV news and more so if these calculated actions against the employers concerned will detrimentally affect the business, international standing and reputation and tarnish its corporate image. Sometimes a court award or penalty given against a multi-national employer for transgressing local laws and regulations may not militate against its international business as a whole or even its corporate image, because this may be contained and capped at low profile at national or state level. But an infliction by social media or other informal pressure groups could certainly be spilled beyond local and national precinct and inflict heavy casualty on an international business. But on positive note this informal pressure could certainly thwart to a considerable degree any intended injustice, unfairness, exploitation or wrongs against labour force. These are the new, contemporary voices of workers' representation which have seemingly though replaced the trade unions, ringing a death knell to their movement world-wide.

**Future of trade-unions**
But these new, contemporary voices of workers' representation, whether It comes by way of workers empowerment concepts or employers' social accountabilities models or fresh repertoires for labour representation, can never and most certainly will never

replace or take the place of sacrosanct trade union movement. Why is this so?

- They were there for the workers at their most desperate point of need, at the height of labour exploitation and the brutality that labour suffered in their darkest hour in history during the great industrial revolution of classical epoch. Where were the contemporary voices then?

- Trade union was born and cradled with the sole and primary objective of pursuing the cause of the working class and only the working class. In other words, trade union came as a stable, primary food for the working class and not as supplementary intake. Whereas the contemporary voices aids workers cause only as supplementary or an auxiliary matter.

- Traditional trade unionism and its quotidian obligations are discharged within strict confines of formal legal and legislative setting, but whereas these contemporary repertoires are discharged without such institutionalized boundaries, which would be liken to contrast between a formal organization chart and a grape vine organization or a contrast between a conjugal wife or an unwedded mistress or concubine.

Modern day thoughts, whether they are flowery meta-theories or middle ranges theories spawned by modern human resources philosophers, whether it be workers-empowerment-fashions or employers'-social-responsibility-whim and relegating trade-unions and classical industrial relations as outdated vogue all together and at the same time giving credence and prominence to fresh inventories of alternate voices of labor representations, are but built on flimsy foundations of passing gravels. These flimsy meta-theories and insubstantial middle range theories are but a passing vogue and when the popular trend passes off in a cycle that oscillates between inflationary prosperity and downturn recession, the dormant trade-union of classical industrial relations or even of dualistic epoch would soon revive and rebound with renewed fervor in the vacuum thereof. Why is this so? Take for example the axiom- on one hand that the entrepreneurs' are motivated by an innate, inborn seed of greed for profit which cannot be totally rooted out in its entirety by any noble meta-theories however benign it may. And this seed is further germinated or watered by the base animal instinct of the survival of the fittest.  These instincts may be subdued or pacified by the aforesaid meta-theories to a considerable degree of an extended period of time but not rooting out the seeds in its entirety.  The labor on the other hand are driven indefatigably by the survival instinct of their base need for food, shelter and clothing, the base protective coverage for the family and this basic need will never be compromised or short-changed to any considerable magnitude by the aforesaid meta-theories no matter how convincing or noble it might be.

Therefore, when meta-theories and middle range concepts are built on gravel foundations, especially when such are devoid of any consideration of the foregoing axiom, then it should be rightly concluded these are only ephemeral theories built on both passing and shallow foundation. If it appears presently working fine and well, then it is only transient and will soon pass away into oblivion. But trade-unionism will live and thrive on perpetually, because it is premised on the foregoing axiom, taking into cognizance the base, immutable instincts of entrepreneurs and labor force and no amount of fleeting and fanciful new age human resource philosophies is going to root out the base instincts imbedded respectively in this two entities which are perennially opposed to each other. And if this is not so, how would you explain the following Malaysian paradox, which is also applicable universally:

**Amnesty International at a press conference in Kathmandu (Nepal) on 24 March 2010, had this to report:**

Migrant workers in Malaysia are being exploited by both employers and state authorities, according to a new report of Amnesty International. Nepalese Section of Amnesty International by organizing a press conference in Kathmandu on 24 March 2010 launch the report 'Trapped: The Exploitation of Migrant Workers in Malaysia'.

Amnesty International's Asia Campaign Coordinator Robert Godden prescribed the Nepal government to take precautionary measures to ensure safety and protection of Nepali migrant workers. The report says "migrants are often forced into labour or exploited in other ways, such as having their passports confiscated by employers".

A four-member research team had interviewed 200 migrant workers working in Malaysia in mid 2009 to prepare the report:

"There has to be proper cooperation between Nepal and host countries in line with Memorandums of Understanding (MoUs) that guarantee minimum wage rate, maximum working hours, safety provisions, insurance and monitoring of recruitment agencies," Godden stated.

"Most recruiting agencies are found to have lured workers with false promises of high salaries, better working hours and finer provisions. So, the government should ensure that the prospective workers are given the correct information regarding salary, working hours and job responsibility," he added.

The report shows poor condition of migrants from countries like Nepal, India, Bangladesh, Myanmar, Vietnam and so on.

The report recommended that Malaysian authorities must initiate action to end the widespread workplace and police abuses on the migrants workers.

In addition, the report has also urged the respective governments to be cautious and take serious initiatives to save their citizens from being abused and exploited.

The report has strongly objected to the existing system in which employers confiscate the workers' passports exposing the workers to the potential threat of being arrested by police.

"Migrant workers are critical to Malaysia's economy, but they systematically receive less legal protection than other workers," said Michael Bochenek, author of the report and AI policy director. "They are easy prey for unscrupulous recruitment agents, employers and corrupt police."

The undocumented workers in Malaysia is worst than of documented. According to its Malaysian government sources, Malaysia has 2.2 million documented foreign workers, almost 20 percent of Malaysia's workforce. Approximately the same number of migrant workers working in Malaysia are undocumented.

The report launched in Kathmandu by the Chairperson of AI Nepal Hem Kumar Khadka and Director of AI Nepal Rameshwar Nepal Informed to the Journalists about the highlights of the report.

**Despite adequate laws to protect migrant workers, why they continue to suffer**

[1]Workers for McDonald's in Malaysia say they were victims of labour exploitation

**Migrant workers employed through labour supply firm allege they were deceived about wages, cheated of payments and had passports confiscated unlawfully**

 A McDonald's logo is seen in a restaurant in Shah Alam, outside Kuala Lumpur. Migrants say they suffered labour abuses while working in the firm's restaurants in Malaysia.

Workers at McDonald's restaurants in <u>Malaysia</u> claim they earned as little as 60p an hour and were cheated out of months of salary, a Guardian investigation has found.

The workers allege they were subjected to months – and in some cases years – of exploitation by Human Connection HR, a labour supply company contracted by McDonald's in Malaysia to provide workers to its restaurants in Kuala Lumpur.

The workers, who come from Nepal, say they had their passports confiscated, in contravention of Malaysian law.

They claim they were deceived about their wages and were charged additional fees when they arrived in Malaysia, resulting in a 25% deduction in their basic

---

[1] Source: The Guardian- international edition, 28 Nov 2016

monthly salary. Over the course of working at McDonald's, this equated to the loss of months of wages.

Unlike in its other major markets – including the UK and US – where McDonald's operates through a franchise model, McDonald's outlets in Malaysia are company-owned.

The migrants also say that their salaries were not received on time, leaving them unable to buy food or send money home to their families.

 "We didn't have the money to eat because we were not paid regularly," said one man, adding that some workers went on strike earlier this year in protest at late payment of wages. "How can we go to work on an empty stomach? I thought it was a good company and I would earn good money. Now my life is damaged. I feel that I have no future."

McDonald's Malaysia said in an email that it had ended its contract with Human Connection. "At McDonald's Malaysia, the welfare of staff is a top priority," said the company. "Earlier this year, we became aware of certain circumstances relating to services provided by Human Connection HR which were not in compliance with our standards. As a result, we have terminated our contract with them."

The investigation, which comes just days after the Guardian exposed allegations of abuse among migrants making products for Samsung and Panasonic in industrial zones across the country, sheds further light on the malpractice of some labour supply agencies used by major international brands in Malaysia.

"We were not given our salary on time," said another Nepalese worker. "When we went to meet the managers of McDonald's to complain, they usually said we were not employed by McDonald's and they are not responsible for anything. One of my friends even went to the McDonald's manager crying after he heard news of his child's death [at home in Nepal]. He asked him to ask for his passport [from Human Connection, so that he could attend the funeral,] but the McDonald's manager said that he cannot do anything. I would rather die than go back to work at McDonald's. I will never work there [again]."

 McDonald's Mid-Valley in Kuala Lumpur. Migrant workers employed here (not pictured) claim they were paid erratically by the labour supply firm that hired them. Photograph: Pete Pattisson

The Guardian spoke to 15 Nepalese workers formerly employed at four McDonald's restaurants in the capital, Kuala Lumpur. The men worked at McDonald's at different times over the course of three years.

More than half said that they had been forced to run away from their jobs without their passports or back pay, entering the illegal work market in an attempt to make some money. This would leave them vulnerable to arrest and detention by the Malaysian authorities.

Others said they had been forced to pay their own way back to Nepal after their passports were not returned by Human Connection.

Some of the workers criticised McDonald's for failing to respond to complaints **of mistreatment by Human Connection while they were working in McDonald's** outlets.

They claim that they repeatedly informed the company about problems relating to wages, salary deductions and passports, but received no assistance.

"I complained about our salary to McDonald's many times, and the branch manager … sent the message to McDonald's headquarters," said one worker. "[But] McDonald's said they had already paid Human Connection."

The manager of one McDonald's branch that previously employed some of the workers claims that the company's headquarters in Malaysia were informed about the problems the men faced: "The labour supply company withheld two to three months' wages. The workers only had a photocopy of their documents, but they should have had the original with them. We are humans. We tried to help them with food, but you can't do it all the time."

During their time working in McDonald's restaurants, the men claim they were paid less than they were promised in Nepal. In some of their contracts it states that they would not have to pay the foreign worker levy, a charge placed on companies using migrant labour in Malaysia that is often passed on to the workers themselves. Payslips seen by the Guardian show that the levy was deducted, however, equating to a 25% reduction in their basic wages.

The workers also claim that they had their passports confiscated by the labour supply company on arrival in Malaysia, a pervasive but illegal practice that ties them to their employer and denies them the freedom to leave their job or the country.

"The supply company took our passports, but they will not send workers back to Nepal or give our passports back," said one man formerly working at a McDonald's restaurant. "Even those who finished the three-year contract cannot go home because they don't have their passports."

Another worker said: "Even when it is time to go, the company does not return your passport. I don't know why … I asked to go home, but the company said they will not send me back."

The workers who chose to return home have had to pay the equivalent of two months' basic wages to a middleman to arrange the documents and paperwork needed to get them back to Nepal without their passports.

"I expected to earn money here," said one. "But I'm leaving with nothing."

The men also complained about the conditions they faced in the accommodation provided by Human Connection while they worked in McDonald's restaurants.

A hostel used by Nepalese migrants working at McDonald's in Kuala Lumpur. The workers say up to 18 men shared the space, with most sleeping on the floor.

The Guardian visited one squalid hostel with paint peeling off the damp walls. McDonald's advertising banners were used as makeshift curtains. In one room, a McDonald's trophy was propped up on a fan switch with "Best of the Best Kitchen Crew" printed on its base. At one point, the workers say, 18 men were crammed into the small flat, with most sleeping on mattresses on the floor. They shared one small, grimy toilet, which also passed as a washroom.

In a statement, McDonald's said: "While local employees make up the vast majority – more than 90% – of our workforce, we sometimes work with established recruitment agencies which employ foreign workers, and sub-contract a number of them to McDonald's in Malaysia. These staff members are employees of the recruitment agency, not McDonald's.

"McDonald's Malaysia made repeated attempts with Human Connection HR to investigate and verify issues of non-compliance shared by the workers, raising our serious concerns through both verbal and written correspondence. Because the workers are not employees of McDonald's, our efforts to address the issues were unsuccessful, as were proposals for McDonald's to assume responsibility for paying workers directly. In the interim, to assist, we authorised restaurants to provide food and provisions to workers affected while we worked to address the issue.

> "Following the termination of our contract, the workers remain employees of Human Connection HR and as such we understand that they will either return to their home country or be redeployed to other businesses."
>
> Human Connection did not respond to a request for comment on the worker's allegations.
>
> Aidan McQuade, director of Anti-Slavery International, said businesses must no longer hide behind codes of conduct but should instead take proactive measures to ensure they are not profiting from exploited labour.
>
> "The great tragedy about this kind of exploitation is that it is actually easy to fix," he said. "Companies operating and profiting from their business In places like Malaysia can't say that they are not aware of the issues facing migrant workers there. They need to take a proactive investigative approach to ensuring that, if they use labour supply companies, those companies are adhering to the law and corporate codes of conduct. It's time for this to stop."

The principal reason is that these foreign workers are ignorant of their rights under Malaysian law. This is understandable, as most of them are barely educated and have opted for menial labour, depending helplessly on unscrupulous recruiting agents, foreign employers and foreign countries to escape starvation and hardcore poverty at their native lands.

Furthermore, these foreign workers are not allowed to form unions. Fears of employers have prevented them from reporting any mistreatment to relevant authorities and they continue to suffer silently, stoically enduring the miseries of exploitation for the sake of sustaining their dependents back in their native lands. This is further augmented by the fact that their passports are usually confiscated by their employers rendering them completely immobile.

At times, when principal employers are unfair and keep up to rules, the outsourcing companies which supplies and manages the foreign workers are unscrupulous, like for example in the foregoing case with McDonalds.

The labour department, the only government agency to monitor the employment situation of foreign workers and to keep a tight monitoring on employers so as to preclude any form of mistreatment of foreign workers, sadly has not expanded and grown at a rate the foreign labour force has grown and expanded in Malaysia.

The Malaysian Immigration and Police departments are plagued by the burden of massive undocumented illegal migrant workers in the country and as result even genuine legal migrant workers are not given the benefit of doubt during inspection and checking of passports especially when these legal workers could not produce originals but just photo-copies of passport and work-permits.

In the meanwhile, Malaysia as petroleum and gas producing nation, with booming construction business and one of the leading producer of palm oil, with growing manufacturing sector continuously demand for more and more foreign labour. And on the other hand there are poor nations ready to offer willing labour force and the climate being ripe for a massive influx of both legal and illegal migrant labour into Malaysia. Where local workers abhor certain jobs that are considered blue collar, dirty, dangerous, hard and menial, foreign workers both legal and illegal excitedly offer their labour for much lower price, thus falling prey to ravenous hiring agents, greedy employers and to corrupt government officers where illegals are smuggled in and exploited.

Where likes of the foregoing McDonald case are but a tip of an ice-berg where the massive underneath of actually exploitation and untold agonies and tragic hidden miseries of migrant workers go unreported and unnoticed by the general populace of our nation.  These unsung workers toil day and night to erect our towering monument of high-rise buildings, majestic bridges, scenic highways, six-star hotels across the nation's coastal resorts and highlands as our middle-class and upper middle-class Malaysians gloat and fight over trivial political, religious and social issues blown out of proportion. Where human dignity of migrant workers is reduced and considered much less than a local Malaysian because of sadistic greed.

McDonald is a global business outlet, modelled and groomed by the new age philosophy, with its flourishing business worldwide, is an outstanding quintessence for workers empowerment models and an excellent epitome of world-wide corporate social responsibility programmes. But when we juxtapose this benign display with the above said empirical reality of the Malaysian outlet's classic case of exploitation and bullying of foreign workers, we see an appalling paradox on one hand and on the other hand the ruse of new age philosophy and its trickery to discredit and dislodge trade unions from its rightful and true standing as the only and only one worthy defender of workers' cause for all epochs.

Another reason being, meta-theories or auxiliary-theories of new age sways, even though they hold great convincing or persuasive powers such as to bring about impressive paradigm shifts, so impacting not only employers but labor as well, are outside formal institutionalized structure, and therefore, it will not stand and endure the test of time, or in other words what is not primarily sanctioned by law and enforced and executed by the strong arm government against the institutions concerned, will not stand and withstand the trial of time or the test of empirical reality. Why is this so? Let us take the following empirical example:

**Award No. 998 of 2001- the case of Sitt Tatt Bhd**
*The claimant in this case was an executive- human resources reporting to the senior manager- human resources. The claimant was harassed sexually by her superior. She lodged a complaint with the Company but was ignored by the Company officials who were reluctant to take disciplinary action on the senior manager even though her complaints were very serious. The claimant then resigned on grounds of constructive and filed a case under section 20 of the Industrial Relations Act 1967. There was evidenced shown in court that the Company had condoned the said sexual harassment by its senior manager.*

*In this particular case, the employer Sitt Tatt Bhd had*

- *Failed to heed and enquire into the complaints of sexual harassment reported by its employee.*

- *Breached its implied duty of care to provide safe working environment for its female employee.*

*The latter is a serious and fundamental breach going to the very root of the claimant's contract of service. And she acted immediately on the said repudiatory breach by walking out of her employment. The Court gave award in her favour.*

*No doubt, in this 2001 case, the claimant was able to obtain some relief from common law and section 20 of the Industrial Relations Act 1967, but at the following cost:*

- *At the opportunity cost of losing her job since constructive dismissal grounds requires walking out of your employment.*

- *The burden of proof or the onus of producing concrete evidence before the court falls squarely on her.*

- *The hefty legal cost involved in industrial court dispute.*

*By this time the 1999 Code was already in place, (*Part XVA of the Employment Act 1955 has yet to be enacted at the time of this case) *but then it was not effective in forcing the employer, Sitt Tatt to conduct the necessary investigations and inquiry into the sexual harassment matter.*

Employers have to now comply with the following mandatory order because of Part XVA of the Employment Act 1955:

- Conduct an inquiry into complaints of sexual harassment

- Or inform the complainant why he refuses to conduct an investigation into the matter

- Or to conduct an inquiry when directed to do so by the Director General of labour

- Or to submit a report of inquiry to the Director General of labour

If the employer fails to do so he is liable to a fine not exceeding RM10,000.00. Had Part XVA of the Employment Act 1955 been in place then, the claimant in this case need not leave her job but instead could have enforced upon the employer to conduct an investigation and inquiry into the said misconduct of the senior manager and would have most likely removed him either by way of dismissal or transfer, considering the seriousness of the offence.

A Dualistic Industrial Relations

The 1999 code, no doubt, had great influential powers to convince and persuade an employer to adopt a policy to *provide safe working environment for its female employee but yet it fell short in effectiveness. Because, any practice or policies carried out outside the confines of an institutional structure is bound to fall short. That would be analogous to saying, the aforesaid new age ideas, that is* workers empowerment and employers' social accountability ideals including fresh repertoires for labour representation, even though we see these abounding all around, *but they are bound to fall short because* these are *carried out outside the confines of an institutional structure.* And we conclude this truism by asserting- despite the flourishing boom of new age ideas, purportedly replacing trade unions, the immensely exploited foreign labor in their current untold misery are going to come running to the arms of trade unions to seek help. For a short moment in their myopia, laboring workmen had spurned trade unions in favor for chimerical ideologies like workers' empowerment *programmes and employers social responsibility ideas. But soon this myopia is going to fall off and they are going to return to the institutionalized frame-work of trade unionism and traditional industrial relations once again. But a return to which class of industrial relation? Classical, Dualism or Unitarian?*

While Classical industrial relations stands on a one extreme end, where employers and employees refuse to behold beyond their respective selfish wants, rights and agenda, the Unitarian industrial relations stands on the other extreme end in totally subduing and overwhelming labour force and is therefore no longer relevant in today's era of globalization of industries, globalization of supply chains, trans-national and trans-continental employment / recruitment net-works and International Framework Agreements by MNCs in their quest to forge new global working relationship with labor. And this calls for the relevance of a Dualistic industrial relation, where there is a strong mutual recognition and acceptance by both parties.

And the future belongs to this relevance- the Dualistic industrial relations with a strong and active moderator, the government. And the governments of nations across the globe have a bounden duty to breathe life to this relevance and in particular to Trade Unionism. Because, history demonstrates when trade unionism dies out, that is when the menaces of religious extremism, global terrorism, human trafficking and exploitation of labor and all manner of current day evils as reported dolefully by our media fill the vacuum.

**2**
## What Is An Institutionalized Industrial Relations & The Theory Of Dualism

According to Kapoor, he stretches further the concept of industrial relations by saying it is a developing and dynamic concept, and does not limit itself merely the complex of relations between the unions and management, but also refers to the general web of relationships normally obtaining between employees, a web much more complex than the simple concept of labour-capital conflict-Kapoor T.N. (Ed.), Personal Mgt. & Ind. Relations in India, 1968.

In a nutshell, industrial relations is not just about working relations between workmen's union and management and resolving conflicts between the two parties. And delving deeper, let us see what is institutionalized industrial relations is all about.

An institution can be defined as

- an establishment or a foundation or even an association, fellowship or a leaque or a union.

An institution can also be defined as

- A long established custom, norm, tradition, convention, idea, concept or habit.

An institution has perpetual life and continuity and its leaders or its management can be replaced.

An institution has its own rules and regulations and by laws including unwritten laws and customs.

At times the state or the government backs-up or supports these institutions through financial, enforcement and other forms of aids to further strengthen these institutions so as to extrude maximum benefits from it.

When we say, for example, the <u>institution of marriage</u> in a society, it goes deeper than a union between a man and woman. There are strict rules of marriage, strictly followed and strictly enforced by general consensus in a particular society and the culture of that society. If you so wish to get married and to be a part of this particular society then it is imperative that you abide by the rules, norms and customs of this institution or failing which you would be ostracized or be totally banished by this particular society.

Here, the institution of marriage means amongst others,

- Strictly a marriage between a single, adult, mature man and a single, adult, mature woman. Anything to the contrary is not acceptable, for example child marriages and marriage between the same sexes or polygamy are strictly forbidden on the pain of total banishment.

- Strictly a marriage solemnized in a recognized and official church and conducted by an ordained minister. Anything to the contrary is not recognized, for example marriage held in a home or conducted by a lay preacher is strictly forbidden on the pain of total banishment.

- Cohabitation between a man and woman before marriage is strictly forbidden on the pain of total banishment.

- And the state or government backs up such a marriage institution by enacting laws, secondary rules & regulation of enforcement and monitoring agencies to aid in the enforcement of the foregoing institution.

And aforesaid **institution of marriage** is structured upon **Biblical theology** so as to reap fruits of happy marriage, to minimize or totally eliminate high divorce rate and illegitimate children, to in-calculate parental responsibility and good family values.

And likewise with **Institutionalized Industrial Relations**, structured and built upon the **theory of dualism** so as to reap fruits of industrial harmony, cordial working relationship between workers and employers, to minimize or to totally eliminate high dismissal rates and unemployment, to in-calculate good work ethics and produce excellent employers. But Institutionalized Industrial Relations could be inclined towards either Classical tendencies or be inclined even towards Unitarian tendencies like for example here in Malaysia, thereby culminating in less than perfect or ideal situations of industrial harmony and suffering workforce, high dismissal rates, high unemployment rates and high crime rates.

**Protagonists of industrial relations**
The two Protagonists of industrial relations are the employers and employees with the government playing a middleman role as moderator where its activities or operations are conducted within the confines of a formalized or institutionalized structure, and that is within the confines of two primary legislations, namely-

- The Trades Union Act 1959 and

- The Industrial Relations Act 1967.

**What are the primary goals of the two Protagonists?**
Firstly, as typical of in any industrial relations or harmony between two opposing entities, that is, the employer on one hand and the workers or workers' union on the other hand and for this relation to gain any traction in a path that is long, dicey and meandering, each entity must by necessity first look beyond their own self-centered agenda and wants to see, understand and commiserate with his opponent's agenda and wants. In fact, isn't this one of the fundamental requirements in dualism? And by way of saying commiserating with the opponent's want, the connotation goes much deeper than even sympathizing at a superficial surface to encompass sublime act of empathizing with the opponent's wants and agenda.

Let us now look at their respective fundamental wants and agenda:

- **Employers on one hand want to minimize labor & safety cost and maximizing working hours so as to optimize profitability of their business.**

- **Employees on the other hand want to maximize their earnings at minimum working hours and enjoy security of tenure.**

- **And the moderator's role is to bring these two forces into an equilibrium.**

A Dualistic Industrial Relations

Industrial disputes or conflicts arise whenever there is a disequilibrium. And the contributory factor to this disputes or conflicts or disequilibrium is when one of the party or even both the parties departs from dualism and incline towards either Classical approach where both the parties refuse to recognize, accept or agree on the opponent's wants and agenda or to Unitarianism where the employer seeks to overwhelm and dominate the other party, which is the labor.

A question may be asked, why call a three party relationship, that is employer, employee and the government, a dualistic relationship?

On the surface it appears to be tripartite or even a multilateral relation rather than a dualistic relation because in addition to the two protagonists we have the whole government machinery, which are the law makers in parliament, the industrial relations and trades union departments, the courts and other conciliatory officers acting as moderators. For example in a badminton tournament we need only 2 players for the game to begin and go on. The game can go on even without a referee. Therefore we have 2 main protagonists over-shadowing the referee, with the referee remaining under the shadows of two shining star players. But the referee certainly makes the game more effective. And likewise, even without government involvement the game can still go on between an employer and employee, but it will not be effective and smooth. Hence the definition- A Dualistic Industrial Relations in a game between two shining stars, the employer and employee and the government acting as referee but remaining in background, playing an effective role in moderating the relationship between the two protagonists.

**Fundamental Structure of Institutionalized Industrial Relations**
Let us now see what the fundamental equation of Institutionalized Industrial Relations is:

| |
|---|
| **Institutionalized Industrial Relations = Dualistic Industrial Relations = Sub-Agents of dualism** |

Employment-Justice & security, fairness and equity can only be found within the purview of Institutionalized Industrial Relations. Dualism, is what gives life and breathe to Institutionalized

Industrial Relations. And the enforcement agents act as pillars of support to Dualism:

- Trade Union legislation

- Industrial relations legislation

- And the Industrial courts

Whereas employee relations with all its persuasive sub-agents of, the Workers empowerment notion, Employers' social accountabilities notion and the Fresh repertoires for labour representation grossly lacks the enforcement agents In the aforesaid equation and therefore cannot be a part of the equation.

For example, under Institutionalized Industrial Relations or dualistic industrial relations for the matter an employer whether he likes it or not or whether he is agreeable or not is forced to accept, agree and act in compliance to the legitimate rights of a worker or to a legitimate rights of an association of workers' union and work along with. Or otherwise face the pain of penalty. Correspondingly, the association of workers' union, whether they like it or not whether they are agreeable or not is forced to accept, agree and act in compliance to the legitimate rights and prerogative of the employer and work along with. Or otherwise face the pain of penalty. And again this is something which employee relations with all its persuasive sub-agents of, the Workers empowerment notion, Employers' social accountabilities notion and the Fresh repertoires for labour representation cannot boast of.

The fundamental structure of Institutionalized Industrial Relations would be analogous to that of perennial medical science vibrant and established and that of employee-relations with all of its sub-agents would be analogous to an ephemeral alternative medicine which appeals to the fancy of certain segment of the general populace for a time being and then takes a plunge down headlong like a passing fade. But the pillars of dualism are a sure foundation, withstanding the acid-test of time and history. And employee-relations with all its persuasive notions but void of enforcement power and the acid-test of time and history as aforesaid can certainly complement and add its auxiliary support to this sure foundation which has withstood such acid-test but certainly it cannot take its rightful place as sure foundation. And furthermore, employee relations does not have as much institutional support by the state as industrial relations.

Therefore, the sub-components of the term, "**Institutionalized Industrial Relations**", amongst others are,

- Industry or inventiveness and

- Working Relationship between employers & employees.

- And such a relationship of enterprise supported and moderated by the state or government by way of structured institutions of labour & industrial laws, trade union laws, various conciliatory departments providing assistance and support both to employers and employees including the industrial courts.

- And lastly but not the least, it is important that we also include the auxiliary arm of modern HRM theory, which has been institutionalized as Human Resources Development Fund (HRDF), to further complement and fine-tune the principal institution of industrial relations.

**Theory of dualism**
Dualism assimilates the following **key notions**-

- That no entity, that is the employer nor the labor should dominate and overwhelm the other, and mutual rights and entitlements of both parties has to be recognized and fully accepted by each other,

- While the moderator, which is the state, should not be passive as in the case of Classical industrial relations, founded upon Adam Smith's **laissez-faire** theory, but rather take on a proactive role; strengthening the weaker party, that is the weaker Protagonist while pacifying the overbearing party, that is the stronger Protagonist and

- Where conflicts arise, then keeping such conflicts within acceptable norms.

- Conflicts between the two parties arise when there is a disequilibrium in the relation of dualism and are resolved when such disequilibrium is eradicated.

The **key elements** of dualism is where both employers and employees **mutually accept** and **agree**;

- The right of the other party to exist and to pursue their legitimate agenda and want,

- The right to disagree and both see industrial conflict as both an evitable and acceptable norm,

- The right of the parties to form union (what is competent and legal) and to be represented by union in a dispute, that is, both the employers and employees.

This is where the exceptionality and the uniqueness of the aforesaid Malaysian legislations, as shown and elucidated in the succeeding chapters- the Trades Union Act 1959 and the Industrial Relations Act 1967 comes to the forefront, blending perfectly against the theoretical notion of Dualism.

But exceptions could be seen in some areas for example by virtue of section 5 of the IRA 1967, it becomes incumbent upon employers to legally recognize and accept the following rights of workers:

- The right to form a union and join union

- And employers are precluded from frustrating this right contractually, that is, by way of inserting a clause in employment contracts preventing workers from joining union.

- Or conversely, employers are to refrain dismissing union workers.

What the foregoing section 5 of IRA 1967 does is that it tells and forces

- deviating employers to return to the path of dualism.

Correspondingly, by virtue of the Trades Union Act 1959, the moderator seeks to streamline union formation and union activities in a methodical manner such as competency and legality of representation in the industry concern. No employer would be inclined to accept a union which is not competent in the industry where the employer's business is run, nor would be the employer comfortable to work with an illegal union.

In other words, what the TUA 1959 does is that it tells, guides and forces

- deviating workers' union to return to the path of dualism.

**What dualism recognizes and what it does not recognize**
The two protagonists which dualism recognizes are the employers and workmen or the respective unions and hence both should be given equal treatment and importance.

And in respect of the latter, in dualism, both legal workers and illegal workers or aliens are recognized and given equal treatment provided the latter is not inclined towards any criminal tendencies save and except the latter's only goal is to earn a honest livelihood. Hence the latter, should not be precluded from any humane covering by a legal Trade Union.

Dualism also amongst others, in line with International Convention on the Elimination of All Forms of Racial Discrimination (Icerd), does not recognize any employment or any preferential treatment in employment on the basis of race, colour, caste, creed or religion.

Dualism does not recognize or condone a state or a government with lackadaisical control over its employers, workforce, trade unions and economy as in free economies, but dualism supports full and strong state control over the foregoing as responsible behind-the-scene moderators, rendering equal treatment to the Protagonists of industrial relations.

In dualism the moderator should always remain impartial and detached and should never play the roles of trade unions as the case with socialistic governments nor take on the roles of private sector employers / entrepreneurs.

In its all-inclusive role, dualism also recognizes and incorporates modern human resources theories to steer and drive the principal institution of industrial relations.

**Why dualism perfectly adapts to Institutionalized Industrial Relations**
Institutionalized industrial relations as contrast to informal employee relations is backed-up by **sub-agents** of Institutionalized Industrial Relations such as;

- the sanction of law,

- legislation and statutes and huge formidable government agencies like labor and industrial relations departments,

- court structure namely the labor and the industrial courts

- and the police-force

as rudiments of enforcement-structure to infuse life, authority and power into what we would call- Dualism.

But whereas the other, that is employee relations, which is backed-up by flimsy shaky ground of persuasive human resources ideologies, theories and philosophies void of any enforcement sanction of law, legislation and statutes and huge formidable government agencies, court structure and police-force would be a mere passing fade and most certainly would not withstand the test of time and history.

For example, a Human Resources Management (HRM) theory inclined more towards Unitarianism dictates:

- Ideal employment relations should be based on enhanced cooperation between the employer on one hand and employee on the other, being motivated to add value to the organization. Such employment relationships are considered as being based on management practices based on informal trust, fairness, knowledge and understanding of employee aspirations and attention to "employee voice" obtained through a variety of channels (e.g. employee and union representatives involvement and participation), as if this would be a potent panacea to cure all industrial disputes, employment problems and bring about industrial harmony,

- Where either one party, that is either the employee or the employer refuses to cooperate or agree to the foregoing ideals or for instant the employer backs off, a reality proven in many a empirical situation involving employees and employers especially in a contractual relationship akin to an asymmetrical relationship.

- In an asymmetrical relationship, there is a strong inclination for a stronger party to subtly exert and dominate the weaker party and therefore the former would merely accord a mere superficial recognition to elements of trust, fairness, knowledge and understanding of employee aspiration as elucidated for example in the case of Lilly Industries (M) Sdn Bhd and Billy Wayne Selsor, Industrial Court award no: 1191 of 2006. When the claimant was unfairly dismissed in this case, the Workers empowerment notion, Employers' social accountabilities notion and the Fresh repertoires for labour representation did not come to the dismissed claimant's rescue. What came to his rescue was institutionalized industrial relations.

In the foregoing case of Lilly Industries, the court had averred that for a just and fair dismissal:

- There must first be a bona fide situation of redundancy,

- Secondly, the workman must be correctly and properly selected for the said dismissal based on LIFO principle,

- And lastly, whether the employer had adopted an impartial procedure in carrying out the said dismissal.

But the court found otherwise in this case, where the employer had breached and defied all three principles as stated above and the court rightly gave an award in favor of the dismissed claim, because the employer had acted in bad faith.

Now, this would be a typical occurrence in a contractual relationship which departs from dualism, especially when the stronger party seeks to dominate and overwhelm the weaker. Now, be this pertinent questioned be asked, and that is, what has become of all that management practices based on informal trust, fairness, knowledge and understanding of employee aspirations and attention to "employee voice" obtained through a variety of channels (e.g. employee and union representatives involvement and participation)?

Why engage the assistance of dualism agents such as the industrial courts and the industrial laws in resolving industrial conflicts in deference to modern human resources theories and thoughts if the latter is found to be far more superior to the former? An appalling paradox, providing food for some profound thought! Now coming to the question, why dualism perfectly adopts Institutionalized Industrial Relations? The answer is because of the aforementioned sub-agents, which perfectly backs-up and supports dualism. Whereas for Classical industrial relations, since it is premised upon laissez-faire philosophy, it does not favor the interference of the aforementioned sub-agents. And for Unitarian industrial relations, due to its domineering characteristics it displays its abhorrence to the aforementioned sub-agents. Therefore, only Dualistic industrial relations perfectly blends with the aforementioned sub-agents.

**How dualism affects an asymmetrical relationship**
Dualism will never be effective in an asymmetrical relationship, but rather it corrects an asymmetrical relationship. In dualism as far as industrial relations is concerned there is no such a thing as an asymmetrical relationship between the two protagonists, that is, between an employer and workmen. But rather it is a balance or a symmetrical relationship. Now, how do we reconcile this appalling paradox between the theory of dualism and empirical industrial relations, a classic paragon of an asymmetrical relationship?

Let us consider the following hypothetical situation:

Within a small, medium sized industry, an employer starts up a small sized metal-toys manufacturing business and employs 50 workers to operate the business successfully. Here initially, the employer obviously overwhelms the workers, as the employer is in a much stronger position then the workers. Then the workers synergized with each other and joined a national union. Thereafter the national union obviously overwhelms the employer. In this first example, we have a situation of an asymmetrical relationship.

Let us now consider the following hypothetical example where a moderator is driven by dualism:

In the foregoing example, the moderator or the state in pursued of dualism,

- Precludes the said workers from joining a national union and instead allows the workers to form an in-house union only, thus creating a symmetrical relationship between the two protagonists or least near perfect symmetrical relationship.

Or

- In the event the workers are permitted to join a national union, the weaker employer is then permitted to join the employer's national union so as to reach a symmetrical relations between the two protagonists.

Let us consider yet another example where the moderator is inclined towards Unitarianism or displays a subtle aversion towards trade unionism:

- In the foregoing hypothetical example, the moderator who is more inclined to protect this small, medium sized employer, precludes the said union formation by workers, that is, neither allows the workers affiliation with a national union nor to form an in-house union, thus creating an asymmetrical situation or a power disequilibrium between the two protagonists with the employer having a upper hand. And because of the moderator's action as such, there would be a culmination of all sorts of social evils and injustices for the working class and their families.

The following New Straits Times report would be a classic empirical example,

- when the state and its institutions are swayed and driven by Unitarianism and Dualism is ignored,

- especially, when there is a strong aversion and lack of full recognition for trade unions (the trade unions are given just a superficial recognition).

---

Wednesday, 7 November 2018, 9:27 AM

# NEW STRAITS TIMES

ESTABLISHED 1845

## 49 Indian nationals alleged forced labour at construction site, escape while guards are away for Deepavali

By Mohd Azam Shah Yaacob and Nurul Hidayah Bahaudin - **November 6, 2018 @ 8:08pm**

KUALA LUMPUR: Forty nine Indian nationals were rescued following an allegation of forced labour at a telecommunication tower construction site in Bentong, Pahang.

The predicament of the victims, who are all men, came to light after they sent a video to friends and family in India crying for help.

Sabai assemblyman D. Kamache said the victims claimed that they were forced to work without salary by their employer.

She said the victims said they were also threatened to be beaten up and sent back to their country in body bags.

She said the victims, who managed to flee the site and sought shelter at a temple in Batu Caves, would be sent home soon.

She said in the video which lasted four minute and 38 seconds, two of the victims claimed their employer had forced them into labour work without salary and prohibited them from returning to India.

"The video was forwarded to the authorities in India who later contacted its high commission here to carry out investigation and rescue the people.

"On the same day, seven men managed to escape, while 42 others fled on Sunday.

"They managed to escape after learning that the site security guards were away for Deepavali celebration," she said when contacted today, adding that he had met the victims at the shelter.

> "During the meeting, the victims told me that they were no longer interested in working as their welfare had been neglected.
>
> "We are working with the police, Immigration Department, Labour Department and the High Commission of India to investigate the claims and work on the process to send the victims home," she said.
>
> Meanwhile, Pahang police chief Datuk Mohd Zakaria Ahmad said a report was lodged today over the incident.
>
> "We will have the statement from the employer recorded to facilitate investigation.
>
> "The case is being investigate under 13 of the Anti-Trafficking in Persons and Anti-Smuggling of Migrants (Atipsom) Act 2007," he said.

And in conversely, let us say, in the foregoing asymmetrical relation, where to the detriment of an employer, the workers union overwhelms and intimidates the former or in other words, to once again in defiance of dualism the state and its institutions are swayed and driven by a strong aversion this time against the entrepreneurs. An adverse situation will once again culminate in the form of business closure and mass unemployment. Because of the resulting disequilibrium in the power balance of the protagonists.

Therefore, when the state and its institutions are driven by dualism, asymmetrical relationship between the protagonists will give way to symmetrical relationship, and the resultant equity and social justice.

Let us look at another example driven by dualism:

---

**Law On Employment Dismissals- 1ˢᵗ Edition, Pg 251, Chp 22**

**The case of Hitachi Consumer Products**
For example in the **case of Hitachi Consumer Products**[2] the International Metalworkers Federation (IMF) had alleged that the Malaysian Trades Union department had denied the fundamental rights of the employees of Hitachi

---

[2] Source: ILO, Definitive Report - Report No 281, March 1992
Case No 1542 (Malaysia) - Complaint date: 24-JUL-90

Consumer Products to join the Electrical Industry Workers' Union (EIWU). The Director General had used his discretion under the Trades Union Act 1959 to decide that the Electrical Industry Workers' Union was not competent to represent the electronic industry workers. The Electrical Industry Workers' Union had served a notice on Hitachi Consumer Products for union recognition on 13 November 1989. On 05 June 1990, the Trades Union department responded by conveying to the Company that EIWU was not competent to represent the workers.

Thereafter 1,093 workers of the Company went on strike. The Company and the Industrial Relations department instructed the workers to return to work as the said strike for non-recognition of the Union by the DG of Trade Union was illegal. The DG had merely exercised his discretionary authority sanctioned by law to declare EIWU was not competent to represent the workers. But the workers refused to return and the Company dismissed all the 1,093 workers who had participated in the illegal strike, including 8 workers who were dismissed earlier for instigating the illegal strike. But the dismissed workers except for 21 workers were later reinstated by the Company after they gave a written apology for participating in the illegal strike. The 21 dismissed workers filed a case under section 20 of IRA 1967. But an amicable settlement was reached without going to court with the assistance of EIWU during the conciliation meeting with a settlement amount of 70% of the last drawn salary for every year of service.

The IMF had alleged the earlier 8 workers were dismissed for organizing union activities, which being a legitimate activity sanction by law. Employers cannot dismiss workers for carrying out any work or activity in respect of union organization and such a dismissal would contravene the law. But the government disputed this claim saying the said workers were instead dismissed for participating and instigating in the illegal strike.

By participating in an illegal strike or instigating fellow workers to participate in such illegal strike (and provided it is proven), the worker has just created a legal loophole for the employer to dismiss him.

In Malaysia, the right to strike is a restricted right. For example, section 10 (1) of the Industrial Relations Act 1967 precludes workers from going on strike following a decision on union recognition:

10. (1) **No workman shall go on strike** or do anything which is rendered lawful by virtue of the proviso to subsection 40(1) for whatever reason during the pendency of proceedings under section 9, or after the decision of the Minister thereunder **by reason of any dissatisfaction with such decision**.

What started off in Article 10 of the Federal Constitution of an apparent wide unrestricted right and unfettered freedom of association, has been narrowed down to a restricted right and fettered freedom of association by the Director General of Trades Union (DGTU)'s administrative-discretionary-authority to segregate and draw a wide demarcation between an electrical industry and electronic industry.

The International Metalworkers Federation, being a foreign body could not understand the rationale behind this idiosyncrasy of the Malaysian situation and criticized the Government. As to why the Malaysian government restricted and curtailed the formation of a national union in the electronic industry as compared to the electrical industry or other industries or in the plantation sector.

The electronic industry[3] is a pet industry which the Government attracted from overseas by offering many incentives including a fifteen year unionization ban and thereafter a restrictive unionization control. It is a labour intensive industry and during the decade of 1990's it was a booming business economically for the nation. The electronic products such as LED television receivers, audio visual products, digital cameras and numerous sophisticated gadgets produced by renowned world class American, Japanese and Korean companies contributed significantly to our nation's economy.

Apart from this, these electronic companies also initiated abundant R&D work, particularly to aid global markets. The Malaysian Investment Development Authority reported exports of consumer electronic products in the year 2011 amounting to RM22.36 billion (USD8.7 billion). But above all, these electronic companies were sustaining the livelihood of the lower and middle class people, who comprise of the bulk of the working population of the Parato 80/20 rule. That is why the Malaysian Government as a responsible government did not succumb to the demands of these International Labour Organization and International Metalworkers Federation for unfettered rights to union activity. Or otherwise the detrimental motion of Parato rule as illustrated in chapter 23's hypothetical example 1 would be set into effect.

Here, the Malaysian government (driven unwittingly by dualism at this instant), played a proactive role in nurturing and protecting the infant electronic industry in the nation and came up with a fifteen year ban on its unionization until the said industry took root and strengthened. But even then following the said fifteen year period only in-house unions were allowed for the electronic industry, as

---

[3] Source: Malaysian Investment Development Authority

national union or even an international union like International Metalworkers Federation (IMF) could easily overwhelm this industry. Thus dualism comes to the aid of the weaker protagonist, be it employers or the workers setting both in par with each other and anything less than a balanced, equal relationship is not of dualism.

**Dualism and Trade Unions**
When Prime Minister Margaret Thatcher of the Conservative Party came to power in United Kingdom that is in 1979, she dealt a subtle blow to the might of trade unions and weakened labor movement and strengthened and freed the weaker entrepreneurs. In years preceding this, the might of labor movement was actually overwhelming the entrepreneurs, where wage inflation was high and unemployment rate was lowest. In a situation where labor movement was prominently dominating the full employment scenes in UK and with an inflation rate averaging about 25% during mid-1970s', one could only imagine the type of power trade unions were brandishing over entrepreneurs and the government. And the shift in industrial relations began after 1979. For example, she brought an end to the year-long strike of the miners thus unfettering the weaker mining-entrepreneurs to bring about a dualistic proportion:

One of Thatcher's most heated political battles came in 1984, when the miner's union struck. Earlier in Thatcher's term, in 1981, the miner's almost struck but the government immediately gave in and offered concessions. Thatcher spent the ensuing years plotting to make sure that never happened again, by changing trade union laws, stockpiling coals to blunt the impact of a strike on consumers and even having MI5 agents infiltrate the miner's unions.

So when the miners struck in 1984, she was ready. After nearly a year, the miner's returned to work without any concessions from the government. The National Union of Miners, which just 10 years earlier had toppled the Conservative government of Edward Heath, was permanently weakened.

Next in pursuance of a macro-economic strategy, the Conservative government of Britain went after the inflationary control instead and brought it down. This then adversely affected the full employment boost, thereby weakening the union further, but brought the inflationary rate down and improved the economy.

But here is where Mrs. Thatcher erred, when the general industrial relations status reached a dualistic equilibrium, she continued weakening the unions further and continued strengthening the entrepreneurs further, tilting heavily towards Unitarianism and thus unleashing new evils of monopsony, employment insecurity, poor work conditions and exploitation. Likewise in Malaysia, where trade union movement are weakened and precluded from reaching its dualistic equilibrium, the Pandora box will be opened and we will see chagrin examples of exploitation and human slavery in the likes of the aforesaid 49 Indian nationals.

It would be altogether untenable to say we need to totally eliminate shark species from the oceans of earth just because they are man eaters and have killed quite a large number of our human swimmers. To eliminate these beautiful sea creatures from our oceans would bring about a great ecological disaster and nightmare. In like manner, it is altogether untenable for critics to say we need to totally eliminate trade unions or at least to weaken trade unions considerably in the business world just because they seemingly undermine businesses and investment and disrupt productivity due to strikes and industrial disputes.

**Dualism and Monopsony Power**
Let us take a hypothetical situation of a town with a population of 100 bread-winning miners. A single and only mining company employs and sustains these 100 men in this particular town. If any of these 100 mining workers abandon their jobs and leave, they will never be able to find another alternate employment or a means to survive. Under this situation, the single and only mining company in town is said to wield what we call a monopsony power. This single employer will be able to arbitrarily reduce wage rate of these workers with complete impunity and there is no one to question him. And the likes of which in the real business world can be found in companies holding monopoly and oligopoly business controls and dictate workers' wage rate and general employment terms at their whims and fancies that could be far-fetched from what is fair, reasonable and equitable.

How to counter balance a monopsony power? The answer lies in dualism. And by way of dualism or rather by way of institutions which are driven by dualism, we empower, strengthen and unleash trade unions to counter, whittle and trim away such monopsony powers of entrepreneurs to bring about a healthy equilibrium of industrial relations. One of the ways a trade union deals with an employer who is holding monopsony power is through collective bargaining. A Collective-Agreement attained through a collective bargaining is NOT a contract of employment but rather is an AWARD of the Industrial Court, legally recognizing and sanctioning the entire spectrum of agreed terms and conditions of employment and related contractual relationship between two principal LEVIATHANS- the UNION and the EMPLOYER or the EMPLOYER'S UNION.

Well, it is no longer about little David versus Goliath but rather it is about Goliath versus Goliath. The individual worker surrenders his personal rights to negotiate with the employer on individual terms and conditions of employment so as to secure better and safer working conditions, better terms and conditions and better security of tenure under a collective aegis of a much stronger single entity- the Union. The individual worker when he negotiates with the employer, he normally negotiates from a premise of weakness. But when the Union negotiates it does it from a premise of strength.

It is liken to many weak individual workers synergizing uniformly into a single mighty Leviathan or a single Goliath to faceoff the employer. That is why the primary purpose of a Union formation is to initiate Collective Bargaining with the employer and conclude a Collective Agreement. After which the concluded Collective Agreement is submitted to the Industrial Court for cognizance. After cognizance, the Collective Agreement becomes a principal legal-document from which stems out all contractual relationship with respect to employment, trade disputes and non-compliance matters including conciliation and arbitration between the two parties. And one of the key moderators is the institution of Industrial Relations department.

Dualism does not champion the cause of business entrepreneurs nor champion the cause of labor to the extent of crushing and putting down one in favor of the other. But rather dualism endeavors to attain an equilibrium of power and equal standing between the two protagonists.

**3**
**Early Malaya & The Age Of Dualism**

The Age Of Dualism displayed its prominence during the pre-independent period, that is, during decades preceding 1957, where labour solidarity was at its pinnacle of dominance having its major sway over employment, political, economic and social strata of then Malaya.

In early days, the bulk of the Indians worked at Rubber plantations and to some extent in the government road construction sector. The bulk of the Chinese worked in tin mines and to some extent they were involved in small businesses. While the Malays served in civil service. The workers in the rubber plantations, tin mines and in the civil services began forming or rather what synergized into a single-labour-movement called General-Labour-Unions or the GLU, where membership was open to anyone without restriction to any industry or private or public sector, thus wielding great power, influence and counter-balancing the formidable powers of private and public sector employers- unlike what we see today.

For example, [ii] The Selangor Engineering Mechanics Association which was akin to a workers union was first registered in 1928. And the Pan Malayan General Labour Union was incepted in 1946 and thereafter the All Malayan Council of Joint Action driven by forces of dualism which pressured the moderator, the British Colonial government in Malaya into ultimately securing citizenship for migrant Indian and Chinese workers working respectively in the rubber plantation and in tin mines of yonder days. Where these component unions under the singular General Labour Union representing unionized labour from a wide spectrum of industries, both private and public sectors treading beyond their sacred boundaries of employment carrying the workers' course venturing into forbidden boundaries of socio-economic and political spheres. And the driving force behind this was it not dualism?

**Epic Workers' Strike Of 20 October 1947 Marked The Declined Of Dualism**
A multi-racial alliance with a broad spectrum of workers union and NGOs organized a nation-wide massive strike over constitutional

and other political rights, albeit non-violent. The moderator that is British Colonial government of Malaya then responded negatively by dealing a lethal blow to dualism and opening the flood-gate of Unitarianism to rush in:

- The Pan Malayan Federation of Trade Unions (PMFTU) was then dismantled, de-registered and its leaders detained.

- The Emergency was declared and strict boundaries were set for trade unions to preclude them from entering or taking up any cause of politics.

- The General-Labour-Unions (GLU) was done away with.

- The implementation of the Trade Union Ordinance of 1940 to further enfeeble and undermine the solidarity of labour and trade union rights for the sake of facilitating the British in World War 2;

- Where trade unions under the new ordinance were all required to register with the government a fresh, in a sense now the stronger unions were filtered out,

- The erstwhile affiliation of private sector and public sector union were now segregated and kept apart for obvious reasons,

- Usage of union funds for political cause were now circumscribed if not all together restricted,

- Trade Unions were further segregated into respective occupations and industries.

Post independent governments of Malaysia from the then Alliance to the Barison National right up to the present Pakatan Harapan governments not only simply continued this colonial legacy but weakened labour and trade unions further. It is estimated that only six percent of the nation's labour force is unionized and this figure is on the decline year after year, where it becomes a national taboo and a transgression of legal edicts to mix employment and politics, where union membership or affiliation will be frown upon by a society which keeps abreast with nascent illusive customs that leans heavily towards Unitarianism.

The foregoing slaughter of the GLU in Malaya was in reality akin to a hypothetical slaughter and mass annihilation of apex-predators-sharks from our oceans just because of some fatal attacks on our human swimmers and thereafter to face the full brunt of the resultant ecological disaster in our oceans. So to say!

[iii]**How The British Colonial Government dealt a blow to Dualism**

With the foregoing changes to trade union law mooted by the British Colonial government and its legacy continued to the very letters by post independent governments of Malaysia, federation of trade unions affiliating various crafts, sectors and industries were practically nullified and could no longer be formed. And the newly incepted Malaysian Trade Union Congress (MTUC) in 1949 could no longer be registered as a Federation. Instead the MTUC was registered under the Society's Act, thereby effectively becoming a society for unions bereft of all the rightful functions of a union in a true sense where it no longer has a say or any conspicuous influence over the socio-economics affairs of the nation.

What we see now is a marked departure from dualism:

- Where the primary institutions of labour and industrial relations inclining heavily towards **Unitarianism,**

- Where the already feeble protagonist, that is, the trade union of workers are further afflicted and weaken by the moderator, whereby amongst others, myriad laws and regulations are being enacted and enforced to its detriment,

- While the stronger protagonist, that is the employer, is further strengthened and protected by the moderator,

- And with the advent of GLCs, that is Government Linked Companies or government controlled private businesses, the moderator itself taking the role of the latter protagonist, which is a breach of one of the cardinal rules of dualism.

In all fairness to the British Colonial government, they had to do what they did then was because of the Communist Party of Malaysia or CPM which had manage to infiltrate and influence the Malayan trade unions to a considerable extent. Let us say for argument's sake the CPM had ruled the nation, what would have happened to dualism? It would have certainly militated to the other extreme end diametrically opposed to Unitarianism- that is leaning heavily towards classical or Marxist, once again breaching the rules of dualism.

This by itself would be equally bad as proven by ample empirical patterns of collapse communist nations over the last few decades like USSR, East Germany and several others where the moderators of these respective Marxist nations:

- Where the primary institutions of labour and industrial relations inclined heavily to towards labour and workers union,

- Where private businesses & commerce, entrepreneurs and employers were further afflicted and weakened by the Marxist moderators, whereby amongst others, myriad laws and regulations were enacted and enforced to its detriment,

- This instant where the stronger protagonist, that is the labour force and workers union were further strengthened and protected by the Marxist moderator at expense of the weaker protagonist, the employers,

- And the state owned or the moderator owned or the Marxist government controlled companies taking the role of the former protagonist thus breaching once again the cardinal rules of dualism.

But the British government bestowed upon the trade unions back at home with far more dignity than they did in Malaya. The principal reason being post-war undercurrents of Classical / Marxist gambits and the General Labour Union of Malaya unwittingly opened its doors to such overtures, began organizing massive nationwide strikes over the general working populace's demand for higher tin and rubber prices, cheaper free flow of rice, better working and living conditions and citizenship for immigrant Indians and Chinese.

At the same, during the turbulent post war period, the pre-independent Malayan ground was very fertile and conditions were very perfect for industrial unrest. The socio-political welfare was at its lowest ebb and this was exploited by the Communist Party of Malaya swaying the General Union to the other extreme opposing the Colonial government. And when the Colonial government perceived that their colonial interest came under a threat, they reacted against this, which is the perceived threat:

- The trade union ordinance was further amended in 1947 requiring a re-registration of all unions where general unions were done away with and the said re-registration was only by way of similar trades or occupation, similar industries or sectors,

- In 1948, the State of Emergency was declared over Malaya and the Communist Party of Malaya was banned and outlawed causing the trade unions to become headless and plunge into a slow atrophy.

The colonial government had stop this tendency or a gravitation towards Marxism, but in the process they also dealt an equal blow to dualism in their counter tug-of-war towards **Unitarianism**:

- When the moderator takes sides with workers union and afflict and weaken employers and entrepreneurs, it will be a death blow to dualism,

- And conversely, when the moderator takes sides with employers and entrepreneurs to afflict and weaken workers union, once again it will be a death blow the dualism.

In dualism, the moderator strictly remains detached from both the protagonists, the workers union and the employers and his principal task is to strengthen the weaker protagonist thus creating an equilibrium of power. And in respect to the foregoing the British Colonial government had miserably failed. And the post independent governments of Malaysia have also equally failed.

**Early historical facts of Malaya**

The early Colonial government of Malaya in order to break and detach the powerful trade unions from their active involvement in politics and socio-economic situation of the nation, enlisted the help of a British trade unionist John Alfred Brazier in 1945. He became a trade union advisor in Malaya, with a mission and goal to slowly whittle away the wide spectrum of its involvement and activities as mentioned and to narrow its boundary to strictly employment matters and disputes- a subtle blow to dualism and to off-set the dualistic balance in favour of powerful British business entrepreneurs who were operating the plantations and tin mines and other businesses in Malaya. The foregoing was in stark contrast to the situation back in United Kingdom where trade unions played active role without such narrow boundaries.

The trade unions of Malaya especially the PMFTU contributed significantly to the development of the early Constitution of Malaya but this fact was relegated to a dark corner and hidden from the limelight of history. It became a transgression of law for national union leaders to canvass and meet up with workers at plantation sites and the sacrosanct right to strike was severely curtailed and restricted. Dualism thrives and lives by this fundamental right to stage peaceful strikes in persistence of any trade dispute by workmen. And therefore it would be wrong for the moderator to infringe this right or to restrict it.  For example an article appeared in Malaysiakini:

- In 1947, the ordinary trespassing law was used to keep union organisers from meeting and speaking with workers in plantations.

- For instance in late March 1947, a large police force came to the Dublin estate in Kedah to arrest a federation of trade unions official for trespassing as he was speaking to a group of workers there. When the workers closed ranks around the official, the police opened fire, killing one worker and wounding five.

- In a clash between police and workers at the Bedong estate on 3 March 1947, 21 workers were injured; whereby "the strike leader died of injuries received at the hands of the police a few days later". 61 of these workers were charged and sentenced to six months' imprisonment.

**The Colonial Government & the domestication of the right to stage peaceful strike**
History teaches that the right to stage peaceful strikes including the rest of the other fundamental rights of trade unions should never be domesticated by moderators or even by anyone nor should this role be taken in any proportion by anyone for any noble cause save and except by the trade union of workers.

Why is this so?

For example, let us take a historical example:

In early days during the peak of dualism, it was reckoned to be an inalienable right of worker to stage a peaceful strike and he cannot be dismissed for exercising this fundamental right. Then came a Supreme Court ruling in 1947 which upheld dismissal of plantation workers for staging a strike as justified and for just cause and reason on grounds of breach of employment contract. Another classic example of trade union domestication and a transgression of a cardinal rule of dualism. And what we see today is a timid and an ineffective trade union.

Between years 1347 to 1351 a shocking pandemics swept across Europe during a dreaded epoch known as the Dark Ages. 200 million masses perished in this Black Plague, the worst in the history of mankind. No doctors could help. No scientist could help. The best of medical science and hospitals of that time could not help. And rodents were the carriers of this Black Death as the world stood helpless. Then people brought in wild-street-homeless cats from the four corners of the world into Europe. Because no doctors, no scientist, no hospitals and no medical sciences could deal with these rodents. These wild-street cats then began attacking these rodents, devouring them. And the Black Plague came to a halt and disappeared and Europe was saved by these wild-street-homeless cats. But what do we see today. Domestication of these wild-street-homeless cats into pussy-home-cats. As result today rats and mice are chasing and beating-up these feline pets. If today there were to be another outbreak of Black Plague, rest assured, our present domesticated cats will no longer be effective in dealing with this pandemic. Why is this so? The answer is- Domestication!

Like manner, in keeping at bay the myriad social pandemics of yonder days we had unleashed the "wild-street-homeless" trade unions. It worked well for early Malaya. But when the Colonial government began domesticating the trade unions since 1947 and this legacy continued till this very day by the ruling governments of Malaysia, is it of any surprise we are seeing today some of the worst social plagues of history unfolding before our eyes!

**Social plagues**
Many of the social plagues of contemporary Malaysia have their subtle roots and nexus with the foregoing domestication of trade unions of early Malaya by the Colonial government. For example:

*Sampath Kumar Vellingiri & 78 Yang Lain v Chin Well Fasteners & Co Sdn Bhd,* 2003] MLJU 292
In this case, two middle-men recruitment agents, one local Malaysian and the other from India representing the Malaysian employer were involved. A group of 52 Indian workers from India were hired to work for the Malaysian employer by these 2 agents. The Indian government's requirement for this purpose was for the agent to furnish them with the contract of employment stating the terms and conditions of employment respectively signed by the employer and the individual worker, a power of attorney authorizing the agent on behalf of the employer and the employer's affidavit undertaking proper repatriation of these workers at the employers own expense. With this the 52 workers came to Malaysia. However, when they started to work here in Malaysia they found to their dismay that their actual pay they received was not what they had originally agreed upon, and it was very much lower. These workers had incurred heavy debts in India in order to secure jobs, pay these agents and come to Malaysia. It was then they discovered that they were cheated and filed a case with the Malaysian court and won the case. But their plight was one filled with much brutality to the extent they had to go begging in the Malaysian streets before justice finally prevailed.
Exploitation of foreign workers which is akin to modern day slavery is indeed a social plague. And the only entity fully qualified to arrest this social plague and similar social evils has been domesticated and rendered impotent.

The Bar Council of Malaysia reported the following in its Circular of 28 July 2003:

A Dualistic Industrial Relations

In Malacca, a similar case has recently been brought to court through the Legal Aid Centre of the Bar, involving another group of 45 Indian foreign workers who have been defrauded in a manner strikingly similar to the proven facts in the Penang case. In a separate incident in Alor Gajah, the plight of a group of laid-off and stranded Vietnamese workers is reported (NST, 25/7/03). The State Labour Department director describes their situation as "deplorable" and remarks that those workers "should not be suffering like this". The Bar Council has also received information that a group of Punjabi workers in Ipoh are facing similar difficulties and distress. Other sorrowful tales are from time to time heard, revealing a pattern of shortchanging salary, wrongful deduction of levy, unlawful termination, threat of cancellation of work permit and repatriation, unsafe working conditions without protective equipment, absence of medical attention, and other forms of ill-treatment or deprivation. Yet, these incidents may just be the tip of an iceberg coagulated from greed, inhumanity and the lack of concern.

The Bar Council calls upon the Ministry of Human Resources to immediately conduct a thorough review of the process of recruitment of foreign workers to ensure that they will no longer be susceptible to deception or exploitation in Malaysia. Wherever necessary to achieve that aim, the co-operation of its counterpart in the supplier countries must be sought and obtained. The authorities on both sides must see to it that agreed conditions of employment are strictly adhered to, and that no misrepresentation or deception takes place. Migrant workers, like any others, are surely entitled to be given what was promised to them.

A specialised unit or department should also be set up to assist those foreign workers who encounter difficulties or ill-treatment in Malaysia to seek legal redress. The co-operation of the Immigration Department must be procured to revoke the present practice of immediately cancelling the permits of terminated workers (whether or not the termination is lawful or is challenged) and deporting them. The current practice enables an unscrupulous employer to hold migrant workers to ransom, because the workers can so easily be sent home against their wishes if they attempt to exercise their right against the employer.

The Bar Council further calls upon the Malaysian government to ratify the "International Convention on the Protection of the Rights of All Migrant Workers and Members of Their Families". Such ratification will confirm Malaysia's commitment to be a civilized and caring society which respects human rights.

The Bar Council also urges the High Commissions and Embassies concerned to adopt a more proactive policy, and to intervene and render all possible assistance whenever the rights of their citizens are infringed.

A Dualistic Industrial Relations

Notwithstanding the ILO Conventions on fair treatment of migrant workers including efforts of the government and the Bar Council and other Non-Government-Organisations (NGO) and the Malaysian legislation in protection of these migrant workers, reports of exploitation of migrant employees still appear:

There was a case of a Nepalese restaurant worker who was exploited by the Malaysian employer. The employer kept his passport against his will and did not pay his salary. This Nepalese worker had a valid work permit. Later this worker lodged a complaint with the labour department that he was abused and his wages not paid. He also reported to the Immigration department that his passport was held by his employer without his consent. After this the said worker was arrested during a operation on illegal immigrants when he could not produce his passport. His desperate pleas that his employer is holding on to his passport fell on deaf ears and he was charged for illegal entry and sentenced to 10 month imprisonment and 1 stroke of rotan. The High Court later freed him on grounds that he had a valid work-permit and passport. But this worker by this time had already suffered 51 days of detention and a stroke of rotan.

There was another case of a Bangladesh immigrant worker who was unfairly dismissed by his employer. He lodged a case under section 20 of IRA 1967. Pending the conciliation meeting in the Industrial Relations department, he was arrested and charged for illegal entry to Malaysia. Despite having valid work-permits and valid passports, migrant workers still suffer brutality in the hands of employers and authorities.

The ILO Conventions which Malaysia has ratified has not fully protected migrant workers. During the decade of 1990s, the plantation and constructive sectors suffered severe shortage of labour, followed by the manufacturing sector especially when locals began spurning menial jobs. That's when foreign migrant labour came in droves in rescue these sectors and made a huge contribution to the nation's economy in particular the Indonesians, Bangladeshis, the Vietnamese, Nepalese and other migrant workers. These too have the right to livelihood and human dignity just like any locals.

And in return for their huge contributions to the nation's economy these migrant workers were rewarded with,

- Unsafe working conditions

- Deplorable living and housing conditions

- Discrimination and isolation in the hands of the locals

- Untold horrors of defraud and exploitation

- Inhuman detention at Immigration detention centres

- And a host of other miseries and misfortunes.

But then all is not that bleak, the ILO, the government agencies, the NGOs, the Bar Council, the Legal Aid Bureau, the labour and industrial relations departments, the courts and human rights lawyers are doing all they can to alleviate the plight and predicament of these suffering migrant workers.

No doubt, the foregoing benevolent bodies are doing their utmost best to battle these social evils, but then these bodies can never be fully effective:

- Because as compared to a trade union whose sole business and objective would be only and only workers welfare, the foregoing bodies have myriad other business and objectives.

Let us take another social evil which has become a contemporary or a modern day scourge- religious and fanatical terrorism which has and still is claiming millions of lives globally. The cult of terrorism is diametrically opposed to all and any religious scriptures and practice. With the departure of dualism or rather golden age of dualistic industrial relations and particularly when trade unions powered by dualism died off leaving a vast vacuum, the world then became ripe for this social evil to thrive and expand:

- A unionized worker or when an individual worker is synergized within a unionized covering, he is protected or shielded from all external evil influences as aforementioned otherwise than as an individual where he is more disposed to fall victim to such evil or negative or destructive influences,

- A synergized worker would be constrained or pressured by the unionized group's sole and primary objective to improve one's livelihood or material welfare by way of group pressure otherwise than for pursuing any transcendental pleasures of paradise in the life-here-after offered by religious fanaticism,

- What dualism does to a human mind is to keep it busy and occupied in the pursued of one's livelihood within the context of a group synergy or conversely what would be otherwise convert one's idle mind to a fertile ground for the sowing of destructive seeds of social plagues.

Alas, it was this very protective synergy, the then Colonial government dealt a death blow to and thus unleashing a host of social plagues, plaguing the nation today. And conversely, unleashing a free flow of trade unions, unfettered and in its true form, that is trade unions powered by dualism, would bring about the global demise of the menace of religious and fanatical terrorism and violence. Not to mention, also the demise of other social ills of today.

**Malayan General Labour Unions & labour strikes**
In the trade unionism, there is no regard or consideration for race, colour, creed, caste or religion save the working or labouring class or rather the eighty per centum of the working populace distinguished from the professional class, which is twenty per centum. Take for example the various groups of NGOs which are conspicuously grouped into the various category of races or religious groups as primary objectives of their association. Whereas trade unions are not like this and their only primary objective is the workers' livelihood and welfare. And the only and only weapon unleashed by them to attain their foregoing objective is that of withholding of their labour by way of staging peaceful strikes. Therefore it would be morally and ethically wrong or rather it would be a cardinal sin and transgression of law of good conscience to outlaw or curtail peaceful strikes by a body of trade union in pursuance of their rightful objective.

**Other paperback secular books by B Mathew**

# Fictional Literature

**AMBITION'S PROGRESS PART 1:** A Fictional Allegory
Paperback
Size: 6" x 9"
335 pages
ASIN: 1549706535
ISBN-13: 978-1549706530

An allegory written in flowery classical English of prose and verse. It has abundant allusions, bringing to life and excitement the beauty of classical mythology, western legends, Biblical stories, literature and poetry. This archaic writing of an allegory set in poetical verses may not fit contemporary literature.

This book is a fiction story. But this book is also poetry. And this book is also a philosophy on principles of success. You can read it like a novel or fairytale story. You can also read it like poetry or philosophy.

This allegory is written in classical English language with verses in poetry and allusions. The plot of this fairytale allegory is about a vagabond called Mr. Ambition, who lives in the City of Penury. This city of Penury is ruled by a horrible monster called Lord Poverty. In this city of Penury, this vagabond suffers great disgrace & reproach. One day, a good man by the name of Mr. Think Rich meets Mr. Ambition and encourages him to run away from the city of Penury and escape to another city called the City of Prosperity.

But however, the long journey to that City of Prosperity is filled with great and terrible dangers and deadly snares, where there are many giants, monsters and demons and unimaginable deadly traps. As such, advises Mr. Think Rich, that Mr. Ambition must first make a detour to a mystical labyrinth called the Garden of Sorrow to seek out a mysterious giant called Mr. Other-Self. Because only Mr. Other-Self could safely guide Mr. Ambition to the city of Prosperity.

At the entrance of the mystical Garden of Sorrow, Mr. Ambition meets Mr. Destiny. Mr. Destiny thereafter knights him as Sir Ambition the gallant Argonaut. But however, Sir Ambition finds himself overwhelmed by great misfortunes inside the garden of Sorrow.

Where following a terrible battle with the horrible giant called Suicide, Sir Ambition is captured by the monster, Unemployment and imprisoned in a labour camp called, Hard-Manual-Labour Estate. Here the monster Unemployment maims Sir Ambition by digging out one of his eyes. But with the aid of an alter-ego, Sir Auto-Suggestion, Sir Ambition escapes Hard-Manual-Labour estate, but with Unemployment on hot pursued. In Sir Ambition's search for the mysterious man, Other-Self, he accidently stumbles upon a mysterious kingdom called, the Kingdom of Within.

Here he is welcomed and nursed. After his wounds are healed, the king of this Kingdom of Within and his valiant gladiators escort Ambition out in his search for the elusive Mr. Other-Self. Then once again, the grisly monster, Unemployment confronts Ambition, the valiant king and knights from the kingdom of Within.

## A Dualistic Industrial Relations

But the monster, Unemployment easily overpowers and destroys these valiant men and fatally wounds Ambition, leaving him to die a painful and slow death. But with the help of his alter-ego and others, Ambition gathers his feeble strength and continue searching for the mysterious man, Mr. Other-Self.

Finally Ambition stumbles upon a strange glittering Kingdom of Great-Within and makes a last and final attempt to awaken the mysterious man, Other-Self. Sir Ambition succeeds in setting into motion the awakening process but soon dies from his fatal wounds.

But even though Ambition dies, he dies with anticipated hope of a resurrection from death, knowing that Mr. Other-Self shall raise him up. Part 1 ends with the awakening process of the invincible man Other-Self.

# Employment

**THE LAW ON EMPLOYMENT DISMISSALS**

Paperback: 408 pages
Publisher: Independently published (November 20, 2017)
Language: English
ISBN-10: 1973343606
ISBN-13: 978-1973343608
Product Dimensions: 6 x 1 x 9 inches

The author in his unique style uses hypothetical cases and examples in relation to real life examples to simplify and present a layman treatise what is otherwise complex legal concepts that normally come in verbose and hard to understand legal texts. Readers would be given an understanding and exposition of various spectrum of employment laws within the Malaysian context, including what would be a proper and just dismissal that confines to natural justice and conversely what would be otherwise an unjust dismissal that results in heavy penalty for the employer.

This book would aid both the employees and employers to avoid costly pitfalls in respect of employment contracts, practices and norms.

A newspaper reporter once upon a time approached an old village lady and asked her what would be her preferred job? The old lady then gave a reply that she would rather be a grass-cutter with the government in a low paying secure job than to be top executive in the private sector in an insecure job. This old lady actually speaks for the bulk of the general populace who believe this tale not realizing that a public servant's job is actually the most insecure and vulnerable job as compared to the job in the private sector.

1. **Articles On RETRENCHMENT & DIRECT DISMISSALS**
   Paperback
   ASIN: 1549719637
   ISBN-13: 978-1549719639

2. **THE DIFFERENCE BETWEEN- FRUSTRATION OF CONTRACT & BREACH OF CONTRACT**
   Paperback
   ASIN: 1549700626
   ISBN-13: 978-1549700620

3. **THE RIGHT TO LIVELIHOOD: A Philosophical Essay**
   Paperback
   ASIN: 1549720805
   ISBN-13: 978-1549720802

4. **THE LAW ON CONSTRUCTIVE DISMISSALS**
   Paperback
   ASIN: 1549699296
   ISBN-13: 978-1549699290

# Christian Inspirational Books

**Paperback books**

**Breakthroughs**
**AWAIT IN EAST WINDOW**
A Final Good-Bye To Your Struggles

Paperback: 255 pages
ISBN-10: 1549702246
ISBN-13: 978-1549702242

Breakthroughs Await in East Window

> • Are you caught in a vicious cycle of stagnation, redundancy, frustration & set-backs in your life?

> • Are you constantly hitting walls of hindrances, delays & blockages in every area of your life?

> • Are you constantly haunted & tormented by frustration, disappointments, failures and lack of progress?

The author says, the of life is where you rot and die in stagnation & misery- where you will be overwhelmed by failures, job frustrations, disappointments, hand-to-mouth bondage, lack, misfortunes, constant defeats, closed doors, etc. The majority of Christians are stuck in the West Windows.

Are you facing such hurdles in your life? All these are about to change for you as you read this message and begin your great migration to the EAST WINDOW of your life. The author says, the EAST WINDOW of life, is where you will find success, fulfillment, abundance, happiness, victories and breakthroughs. Find out what is the East-Window of life and how to walk into it and wave a Final Good-Bye to all of your present failures, miseries, job frustrations, disappointments, hand-to-mouth bondage, lack, misfortunes, constant defeats, closed doors, etc.

The author exposes today's popular Spiritual Warfare, Generational Curses & Christian Demonization doctrines & practices as Christian Paganism & West Window bondages. And why Christians need to walkout of these West Window bondages to make a great migration to the East Window of New Covenant Christian Living. And that true Christianity is NOT a ceaseless struggle in spiritual warfare and with generational curses and demons but rather a love relationship with Jesus and new covenant living that is free from all struggles and miseries. This message is written for ordinary men and women walking in the ordinary walks of life; factory workers, office workers, house-wives, Christians etc and all those who presently struggling in mediocre streams of living.

The author recently watched a video clip of a "great prophetic meeting" where a "great prophet" was moving amongst the great crowd of top class businessmen pronouncing billions of dollars channeling into their hands overnight. Every 100% of the prophetic words pronounced were only more prosperity, riches, wealth and glory. Nothing was said about righteousness, sanctification, love, mercies and the forgiveness found through the blood of Christ. Given the reality of life and going by the 80 / 20 rule the bulk of Christian populace do not fit into this prosperity-dreamland projected by these prosperity gospel preachers. This message brushes aside these chosen few blessed ones to reach out and touch the ordinary men and women lost in the ceaseless struggles of life.

As you open your heart to this message, Christ will touch those hidden skills, talents and abilities sleeping within you. These dormant skills will then awake, and you shall then slowly but surely prosper, progress and find success in your career, business and ministry.

**Walking-Out in Mud & Bruises for a Miracle of Reconciliation**
Restoring Divorces, Marital Separations & Broken Relationships

Paperback: 208 pages
Publisher: XLIBRIS (October 3, 2014)
ISBN-10: 1499023685
ISBN-13: 978-1499023688

Do you want healing for your broken relationship and marital breakdown?

In this book, the author says that as you walk out of your room in torn cloth, shriveled hair, and in mud, with black eyes and bruises all over you, your broken relationship, separation, and divorce will be restored and healed by a miracle of reconciliation.

The author addresses today's social disease of marital divorces and separation. Whether you are estranged from your spouse or from your loved ones, your family, your friends, your children, your parents, your church members, your pastors, your business partners and associates, or from anyone, the author avers the eternal truth that there's no broken relationship that Christ cannot heal.

The author speaks about root causes of present-day divorces amongst Christians:

- Affliction of generational curses or spiritual affliction

- One's own inner attitude and mind frame

- Personality traits in individuals:

- Direct attacks and causes by demons

He also shows how to tear down these root causes and bring about miracles of restoration for any kind of broken relationships.

The parable of the prodigal son in Luke 15:11-31 tells you how the younger son became estranged and suffered a broken relationship with not only his loved ones. His own relationship with God the Father was also broken down. But the prodigal son stopped blaming the devil, others, and God and came to his senses. And thereafter, a miracle of reconciliation took place in his life, and there came a happy ending in his life. A happy ending waits for you too.

As you read this book, you too can grasp the revelation of walking out of your room in torn cloth, shriveled hair, and in mud, slime, black eyes, and bruises all over you for the healing of your nightmares of broken relationship, marital separation, and divorce.

# A Dualistic Industrial Relations

**Breaking Strongholds thro' Mid-Night Prayer**
Turning Your Disappointments to Appointments

Paperback: 84 pages
Publisher: Partridge Singapore (May 8, 2012)
ISBN-10: 1482899582
ISBN-13: 978-1482899580

Are you struggling in your prayer life without breakthroughs & results?

Learn what a Mid-Night -Experience is & why it brings about spectacular results & breakthroughs.

Many sincere born again Christians pray & pray, but answers & breakthroughs do not come. Prayers which do not bring answers are NOT effective prayers. And that's why many Christians have fallen into discouragement and have become lukewarm. Christians who cannot experience prayer victories normally run around to preachers, prophets and to gifted men of God for help, in a desperate hope that other people's prayers might help them. And if answers still do not come, they sink further into despair, unbelief and spiritual darkness.

All these are about to change for you as you read this message and begin your MID-NIGHT EXPERIENCE:

- Instead, others will now come running to you for prayer & deliverance

- Your disappointments will now turn to appointments

- You will now live & walk in the supernatural & experience prayer victories like never before.

**Review of Breaking Strongholds thro' Mid-Night Prayer
at Amazon**

**Excellent book....short and to the point!!** July 19, 2016

Pastor Mathew has done a wonderful work by the power of the Holy Spirit in relating the teachings of scripture and how it relates to understanding spiritual breakthroughs in people's lives. Jesus came to save mankind, to destroy the works of the devil so we would have life and that more abundantly. God bless you Pastor Mathew. Your sister in Christ Grace

**Good one!** March 21, 2013

This book is must, to everyone who want answer to their prayer life.

**Five Stars** October 10, 2014

This book really helps my spiritual life. I would recommend it for anyone looking for a good devotional. Thanks

**Information for our times** November 12, 2012

# A Dualistic Industrial Relations

I had this book for a long time on my Kindle Fire before I read it. I have been kept on a fasted life for most of this year and when I inquired of the Holy Spirit what next - I was directed to this book and realised that I would be on a sleep fast for the rest of this year. Talk about revelation!!

**Very interesting** October 31, 2012

This book was different. I enjoyed reading it and got some new ideas from it.I was looking for books with this topic so I enjoyed it but I don't know if others would like it unless they were looking for this topic too.

**What Do You have In Your Hands:**
A Life Transforming Message

Paperback: 34 pages
Publisher: Amazon
Language: English
ISBN-10: 1549746081
ISBN-13: 978-1549746086

This message is written for ordinary men and women walking in the ordinary walks of life; factory workers, office workers, house-wives, Christians etc and all those who presently struggling in mediocre streams of living. The author recently watched a video clip of a "great prophetic meeting" where a "great prophet" was moving amongst the great crowd of top class businessmen pronouncing billions of dollars channeling into their hands overnight. Every 100% of the prophetic words pronounced were only more prosperity, riches, wealth and glory. Nothing was said about righteousness, sanctification, love, mercies and the forgiveness found through the blood of Christ. Given the reality of life and going by the 80 / 20 rule the bulk of Christian populace do not fit into this prosperity-dreamland projected by these prosperity gospel preachers. This message brushes aside these chosen few blessed ones to reach out and touch the ordinary men and women lost in the ceaseless struggles of life. As you open your heart to this message, Christ will touch those hidden skills, talents and abilities sleeping within you. These dormant skills will then awake, and you shall then slowly but surely prosper, progress and find success in your career, business and ministry.

**THE SPIRIT OF PROPHECY- (The God who speaks through Dreams & Visions)**

- Does God speak to people today? The primary means He speaks today is thro' His written Word, the Bible.

- But God also uses a secondary means to speak to you today. And that is, via dreams & visions.

- In this prophetic writing, you will be forced to rethink currently practiced norms, gimmicks and teachings of the materialistic church of today.

- You will learn God's strategies in dealing with coming natural disasters, escalation of crime rates, destruction of marriages, child murders, Extremism, Church splits / crises and others.

- No longer will you stand helpless.

- You will be shown an insight into the spirit world to understand how a prophet of God operates via dreams and visions.

- The author reveals a hidden and mysterious concept buried deep inside the Biblical principle of Tithing, which the present day church has failed to discover.

- Lastly, how to receive and operate in the supernatural prophetic gifting.

# A Dualistic Industrial Relations

<u>**SMASHWORDS ebook TITLES by B Mathew**</u>

1.  <u>Ambition's Progress Part 1</u>

    ***Ebook Price: $0.99 USD. 36250 words. Fiction by*** <u>b mathew</u> ***on August 17, 2011***
    ***ISBN: 978-1-4661-2285-7***

    *An allegory written by B Mathew. Written in flowery classical English of prose and verse. It has abundant allusions, bringing to life and excitement the beauty of classical mythology, western legends, Biblical stories, literature and poetry. This archaic writing of an allegory set in poetical verses may not fit contemporary literature.*

2.  <u>Breaking Strongholds Thro' Mid-Night Prayers</u>

    ***Ebook Price: $0.99 USD. 2350 words. Non-Fiction by*** <u>b mathew</u> ***on August 19, 2011***
    ***ISBN: 978-1-4659-5327-8***

    *Are you struggling in your prayer iife without breakthroughs & results? Learn what is a Mid-Night Experience & why it brings about spectacular results & breakthroughs. Your prayer life will never be the same again. A short Message by B Mathew*

3.  <u>Are You Neglecting Your Soul Today</u>

    ***Ebook Price: $0.99 USD. 6250 words. Non-Fiction by*** <u>b mathew</u> ***on August 19, 2011***
    ***ISBN: 978-1-4660-7992-2.***

    *Are you on the road to Hell Fires? 3 fundamental Gospel Messages of repentance by B Mathew*

4.  <u>Learn to Release Warrior Angels Into your Life's Problems</u>

    ***Ebook Price: $0.99 USD. 2380 words. Non-Fiction by*** <u>b mathew</u> ***on August 19, 2011***
    ***ISBN: 978-1-4661-8464-0.***

*A short message by B Mathew. Are you struggling in desperation today? Your life in total mess, without hope? Unemployment, business failure, debts,troubles? Cheer-up! The God of the Bible will send His mighty warrior angels to deliver you. Learn to release the power of warrior angels.*

5.  *God Can Transform Your Career Life today*

    ***Ebook Price: $0.99 USD. 4850 words. Non-Fiction by** b mathew **on August 21, 2011***
    ***ISBN: 978-1-4659-8304-6***

    *Another life changing short Message by B Mathew. Are you stuck in a job where you are frustrated, redundant, boring, without progress? Make a 180 degrees change by leting Christ touch & anointing those hidden skills within you. And then see what happens next.*

6.  *EAST WINDOWS OF LIFE*

    ***Ebook Price: $0.99 USD. 13060 words. Non-Fiction by** b mathew **on August 16, 2011***
    ***ISBN: 978-1-4660-8550-3***

    *Disappointments & Job-frustrations? Fulfillment & Breakthroughs await in the EAST WINDOW of your life Move away from the WEST WINDOWS- That's where you rot & decay.*

7.  *Restoration of Broken-Relationships, Separations & Divorces*

    ***Ebook Price: $0.99 USD. 23830 words. Non-Fiction by** b mathew **on August 16, 2011***
    ***ISBN: 978-1-4659-0779-0***

    *RESTORATION OF BROKEN-RELATIONSHIPS, SEPARATIONS & DIVORCES DO YOU WANT HEALING FOR YOUR BROKEN-RELATIONSHIP & MARITAL BREAKDOWN? In this book, the author says, as you WALK OUT OF YOUR ROOM IN TORN-CLOTH, SHRIVELED HAIR, and IN MUD, SLIME, BLACK-EYES AND BRUISES ALL OVER YOU, your BROKEN-RELATIONSHIP, SEPARATION AND DIVORCE WILL BE RESTORED.*

8.  *RIVERS OF THE HOLY GHOST*

    ***Ebook Price: $0.99 USD. 2010 words. Non-Fiction by*** b mathew ***on***
    ***August 19, 2011***
    ***ISBN: 978-1-4661-5062-1***

    *RIVERS OF THE HOLY GHOST*

9.  *BREAKING MISFORTUNES & BAD-LUCKS IN YOUR LIFE*

    ***Ebook Price: $0.99 USD. 1990 words. Non-Fiction by*** b mathew ***on***
    ***August 19, 2011***
    ***ISBN: 978-1-4658-3470***

    *BREAKING MISFORTUNES & BAD-LUCKS IN YOUR LIFE*

10. *The God Who Heals All Unpardonable Mistakes*

    ***Ebook Price: $0.99 USD. 1970 words. Non-Fiction by*** b mathew ***on***
    ***August 21, 2011***
    ***ISBN: 978-1-4657-0340-8***

    *Have you committed an unpardonable mistake in life? Let Christ heal you today. A short Message by B Mathew*

11. *Changing Your Disgrace & Shame Into Honour*

    ***Ebook Price: $0.99 USD. 5480 words. Non-Fiction by*** b mathew ***on***
    ***August 21, 2011***
    ***ISBN: 978-1-4661-6568-7***

    *Has the Stars, Fate and Fortune condemned you to a life of disgrace, failure & misfortune. I have Good News for YOU. The Living Christ can turn your disgrace into Honour today.*

12.   *The Spirit of Prophecy pt 1*

**Ebook Price: $0.99 USD. 8630 words. Non-Fiction by** <u>b mathew</u> **on August 22, 2011**
**ISBN: 978-1-4658-5550-3**

 *THE GOD WHO SPEAKS THRO' DREAMS & VISIONS*


13.   *The Spirit of Prophecy pt 2*

**Ebook Price: $0.99 USD. 22870 words. Non-Fiction by** <u>b mathew</u> **on August 22, 2011**
**ISBN:  978-1-4657-0186-2.**

*The God who speaks thro' dreams & visions*


14.   *BE SET FREE- Sinful Addictions, Sickness & Misfortunes*

**Ebook Price: $0.99 USD. 4520 words. Non-Fiction by** <u>b mathew</u> **on September 4, 2011**
**ISBN: 978-1-4660-7381-4.**

 *3 Powerful Deliverance Messages by B Mathew*


15.   *I AM THE ALPHA & OMEGA*

**Ebook Price: $0.99 USD. 6950 words. Non-Fiction by** <u>b mathew</u> **on August 14, 2011**
**ISBN: 978-1-4661-5528-2.**

*Have you felt forsaken by God? Have you felt overwhelmed by Satan? Have you felt your prayers go unanswered? John in Patmos felt the same. But Jesus appeared to John with 3 great revelations. John's life totally transformed and he went on to write the greatest book in the New Testament. Your life too will never be the same again as Jesus comes to you, touches you through the life-changing ....*

<u>Amazon's Complete Selection of B Mathew Books</u>

Discover books, read about the author, find related products, and more. <u>Read more at Amazon's B Mathew Page</u>

**Bestselling Books:** <u>I AM THE ALPHA & OMEGA</u>.

### <u>*AMAZON KINDLE ebook TITLES by B Mathew*</u>

And many more books by B Mathew including kindle version at:

<u>https://www.amazon.com/b-mathew/e/B005EDEMGQ</u>

i https://www.theguardian.com/business/2013/apr/08/margaret-thatcher-transform-britain-economy, https://www.washingtonpost.com/news/wonk/wp/2013/04/08/a-look-back-at-margaret-thatchers-economic-record/?noredirect=on&utm_term=.5793c72728f4

ii
https://www.thestar.com.my/story/?file=%2F2007%2F8%2F26%2Flifefocus%2F20070825194243&sec=lifefocus, Sunday Star, 26, 2007

iii iii https://www.malaysiakini.com/news/402284:
Charles Hector | Published: 17 Nov 2017, 10:52 am | Modified: 17 Nov 2017, 10:52 am